D0389531

MAR 1 8 1993

# PERSUASIVE BUSINESS PROPOSALS

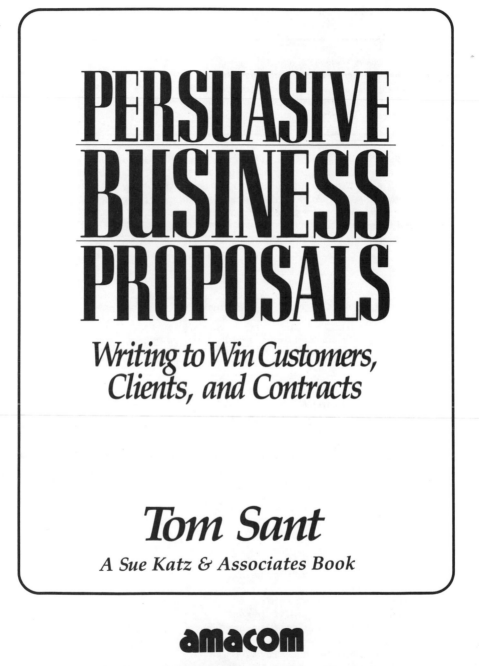

# PERSUASIVE BUSINESS PROPOSALS

## Writing to Win Customers, Clients, and Contracts

# Tom Sant

*A Sue Katz & Associates Book*

**amacom**

**American Management Association**

New York • Atlanta • Boston • Chicago • Kansas City • San Francisco • Washington, D.C.
Brussels • Toronto • Mexico City

This publication is designed to provide accurate and authoritative
information in regard to the subject matter covered. It is sold with the
understanding that the publisher is not engaged in rendering legal,
accounting, or other professional service. If legal advice or other expert
assistance is required, the services of a competent professional person
should be sought.

Library of Congress Cataloging-in-Publication Data

Sant, Tom.
    Persuasive business proposals : writing to win customers, clients,
and contracts / Tom Sant.
        p.   cm.
    "A Sue Katz & Associates book"—T.p. verso.
    Includes index.
    ISBN 0-8144-5100-4
    1. Proposal writing in business.   I. Title.
HF5718.5.S26   1992
808'.066658—dc20                                          92-18963
                                                            CIP

A Sue Katz & Associates Book

Printing number

10   9   8   7   6   5   4   3   2   1

# Contents

# Preface

The goal of *Persuasive Business Proposals* is to teach you how to write winning proposals. Is that something you need to know? Chances are it is, especially if your work involves any kind of entrepreneurial activity, any kind of funded research, or any kind of business enterprise that must sell to other businesses—in short, if your work involves providing solutions for your clients' business problems or meeting their specific needs.

Today, more than ever, success in business requires knowing how to write powerful, persuasive proposals. My clients, from large corporations to the smallest entrepreneurial operations, are all finding that their customers increasingly want it "in writing." As a result, it's now often necessary to write proposals to obtain or hold on to what used to be routine business.

Why? Well, it's partly the influence of the federal government's procurement policies. If you read *Commerce Business Daily*, you know how many billions of dollars are up for grabs each year in federal contracts. Virtually all of that money is awarded on the basis of written proposals. With the federal government the largest single source of contracts in the American economy, government policies and behaviors naturally have an influence elsewhere. Many government contractors, especially those in the defense industry, imitate federal procurement policies and procedures when seeking subcontractors of their own. They require written proposals, and the trend trickles down.

Another factor that's boosted the demand for written proposals is the increasingly complex, technical nature of many of the products being made and the services being offered.

Basic systems and services that people used to take for granted are now the subject of intense competition. An obvious example is telecommunications equipment and service. Since the breakup of AT&T in the early 1980s, the range of vendors and options available in this arena has increased exponentially.

In addition, the business environment has become increasingly competitive. Clients and potential clients who once were willing to make buying decisions based on face-to-face contact are now delaying the decision process, encouraging competition, and—here's the rub—requesting formal proposals from all potential vendors. Clients want to compare sources. They want to study their options. Often they want to be convinced, reassured, impressed. It doesn't matter whether they're buying accounting services or aerospace products, technical writing or touch probe systems. Everything is open for competition.

These are just some of the reasons you need to know how to write a winning proposal. Your job, your company, your prosperity may depend on it. Unfortunately, if you're like most proposal writers, you probably don't have a clue how to do it.

But don't worry. I've taught thousands of people how to write a winning proposal. In fact, I've had people write proposals during our workshops that directly resulted in six- and seven-figure sales.

You can do it, too. This book will show you how.

The solution I recommend is one that I've developed during more than a decade of writing proposals, consulting with proposal teams, and leading workshops on the subject. And it's a solution that has benefited from being tested and proven in the crucible of actual competitive experience. *Persuasive Business Proposals* will help you write better proposals, produce them faster and at less cost, and get the results you want. It will enable you to get the maximum possible return from your investment of time, money, and energy.

During the past fifteen years, I've written more than $11 billion worth of *winning* proposals. In some cases, I wrote the entire proposal. In others, I led a proposal team or facilitated the development of a specific proposal. For some clients, I led classes on general techniques for improving proposal writing skills. The clients I have taught are now comfortably and successfully writing proposals that win contracts, sell projects, gain approval for new ideas, or build relationships.

The methods I advocate have been successful in all kinds of environments, for all kinds of businesses. How can that be? How can a method that produces a winning multivolume, multibillion-dollar aerospace proposal also produce a successful two-page letter proposal to fund a recycling center?

The answer is simple, but it's important. You need to understand it so that you know what to expect. *Writing a winning proposal isn't a matter of content. It's a matter of process.*

I am not qualified to discuss the content of your proposals or those of anybody except myself. I don't pretend that I am. But I don't need to be. You'll provide the necessary qualifications. You're the "subject matter expert" in this project. What I focus on is the process, the techniques of developing and writing a creative, competitive, persuasive proposal.

Not too long ago I received a call from a client in the Washington, D.C., area. The client had been wrestling for more than a month with a request for proposal (RFP), trying to analyze it and to produce a competitive proposal. However, the client hadn't gotten very far. She had figured out what the text margins ought to be and what typeface she wanted to use. She had even found some interesting quotations to use as section headers. But beyond that, she was nowhere. Could I help?

I thought I could. So the client faxed me the RFP's statement of work, and I reviewed it while I flew to Washington the next evening. We got to work at 8 A.M. the next day. By lunchtime, we had the executive summary and technical discussion outlined in detail. By 6 P.M. that evening, these sections had been written and the management section had been outlined. Since the client could write that section herself, I flew home that night.

This story isn't intended to prove how clever I am, but rather to demonstrate how well the method works. If you know how to attack that RFP, if you know what questions to ask, you can do the job yourself.

*Persuasive Business Proposals* is divided into three broad topical areas: general principles of persuasion, project management as it applies to producing a proposal, and the writing skills you need to communicate clearly and powerfully. Here's a summary of each subject area:

- *Section II: A Primer on Persuasion*. At its most basic, a proposal is a form of communication. But its controlling purpose differs from that of a technical memo or a job appraisal. The proposal is written to persuade. As a result, it's vital to understand what persuasion is, how it happens, and what you need to think about when writing a proposal.

- *Section III: How to Manage the Process and Keep Your Sanity*. Developing and publishing a proposal, whether it's a two-page letter or a twenty-volume formal bid, can be maddening. Understanding the basics and having a structured approach to managing a proposal project makes the work much more bearable. The keys to successful proposal management are properly defining the strategy upon which the proposal is to be based and clearly delineating the roles of the people involved in producing it.

- *Section IV: Writing to Win*. You can have the best idea, the best product, the best plan. But if you can't communicate what you have to offer in a way that the decisionmaker understands and accepts, it won't matter how great your idea is. Your choice of words and the way you structure your sentences can either attract or repel the decisionmaker.

I have included examples of both good and bad proposals to help illustrate points about formats, techniques, and processes. The examples aren't there for you to copy and use, although if you want to do that, feel free. But do grasp the principles. Learn the techniques. Understand the process. They can help you write tailored, persuasive proposals of your own, proposals that speak directly to your clients' interests and needs. Proposals that *win*.

# *Section I*

# Why You Need This Book

# 1

# The Challenge You Face

Suppose you're going through the mail one morning and you come across a large envelope containing an RFP—a request for proposal. After glancing through it, you can see that this job is perfect for you. It's one you really want. It's one you're well prepared to handle. All you have to do is write a convincing proposal and win the contract.

No problem, right?

Or suppose you're an account executive representing a vendor of specialized computer systems. You make a powerful presentation to representatives of a potential client and can tell it's gone beautifully. They're extremely impressed. They begin flashing all kinds of buying signals, asking questions, focusing on their particular concerns. Then the chief decisionmaker says, "Well, this looks very promising. Why don't you put together a proposal for us that includes what we've talked about, the pricing issues, and some kind of basic delivery and installation schedule, and then we'll go from there. Okay?"

No problem, right?

One more: You're a partner in a small, local accounting firm. You've managed to grow and develop a solid client base in your region through personal selling to small to medium-size businesses. But now you want to get some larger projects, take on bigger clients, perform complex audits, and generally move the level of the firm's activity up a notch or two. What that means, of course, is that now you'll be competing for jobs against other firms like your own and often against the Big Six. And instead of face-to-face selling, you'll be competing through your proposals.

No problem, right?

Chances are, it *is* a problem. If you're like most people, you find writing proposals a big challenge.

Well, don't feel bad. You're certainly not alone. In fact, some of the very best account executives, program managers, engineers, designers, and consultants—people who are capable of making outstanding presentations face to face and who can manage a program with outstanding success—freeze up when they get back to the office and have to put what they know and what they've recommended on paper. They don't know how to begin. They don't know how to organize their information and ideas. They aren't sure of the format to use, the order to follow, or the language to include.

What's worse, if you're like most professionals, you probably hate writing in general and proposals in particular. That's too bad, because it's hard to do something well if you hate it.

It's true that writing proposals can be a lot of work, and sometimes the effort involves tons of annoying detail that you may find tiresome. But—and I know I'm probably in a very small minority here—proposals are my favorite kind of business communication. They require your best efforts. In writing a proposal, you get to combine your business savvy, your psychological insights, your understanding of language and communication processes, and your creativity, all in one package. When does a mere memo or letter give you the opportunity to do so much? And how often are the stakes so high?

When you write a proposal, you are never certain where it will end up. Will it be read by the manager to whom it was addressed? By a committee of evaluators? By the CEO of the corporation? Your proposal is your surrogate, representing your ideas, products, and services to these people.

Learning how to write powerful, winning proposals can be one of the most important business skills you ever acquire. This skill enables you to communicate your solutions effectively and persuasively to your clients and your colleagues. In doing so, you'll be meeting their needs for information and insight while achieving your own goals.

Besides, writing a proposal is often the most truly professional thing you do.

## Professionals and Writers

Over the years, I've worked with thousands of professionals in companies large and small, in government agencies, in universities, and in health care organizations. One opinion has been voiced more often than any other: "I like my job, but I hate all of the writing I have to do!"

The underlying attitude seems to be that the writing isn't really part of the job. Instead, it's some kind of onerous burden slapped on top of your real responsibilities by a devious or unsympathetic management.

But wait a minute. What are "professionals," anyway? Are they merely people who do for money what amateurs do for fun? That may be true in sports and romance, but not in the business world. No, being a professional means something more, something rooted in the origins of the word.

The first true *professions*—the law and the clergy—arose in the Middle Ages. (In spite of what you may have heard to the contrary, these really are the oldest professions.) Since then, the number of professions has multiplied, but the fundamental meaning has remained the same: A professional is someone who has mastered a complex body of knowledge and who can therefore guide, advise, and tutor others in that area. A professional is somebody who can and does *profess*.

What that means, of course, is that communication is the very essence of the job. It's what separates the professional from the laborer. You expect your doctor, lawyer, technical manager, account executive, or other professional to *communicate*. That's usually not something you expect from your plumber or HVAC mechanic.

All right, so you were humiliated in front of the entire class because you couldn't diagram a compound/complex sentence. All right, so you wasted precious hours of your childhood writing misspelled words over and over again. All right, so you wrote a love note to that English teacher you had the crush on and got it back corrected and graded.

Hey, those things happen.

Isn't it finally time to give up the grudge you've been holding against writing ever since? Isn't it time to approach proposal writing as an opportunity instead of a trial? Believe me, if you're smart enough to master your chunk of the business world, you're more than smart enough to write well. You *can* produce a good proposal, a winning proposal. You can do it! You can even have fun doing it! All you need are a few techniques and a little self-confidence.

# 2

# A Good Proposal Is Hard to Find

I've been fortunate enough to have an interesting mix of clients: Fortune 100 companies, major universities, leading aerospace manufacturers, an international software development company, a couple of telecommunications firms, national and mid-size accounting firms, small manufacturers, R&D firms, consulting firms, import/export companies, a major manufacturer of machine tools, a materials broker, individual researchers seeking government funding, and many others, What they all had in common was their need for help in proposal writing, generally for two reasons:

1. *They didn't have the necessary skills.* Don't misunderstand: In virtually every case, I was working with smart, successful people. But their education and experience hadn't prepared them to write effective, persuasive proposals. Some proposal writers had technical backgrounds and had never been exposed to the basic marketing techniques that could maximize their chance of winning a contract. Others had some marketing knowledge but were using old formats and styles that were cumbersome, overly detailed, and product-focused rather than client-centered. Often these clients ended up writing technical reports, or product descriptions, or company histories, or anything other than powerful, winning proposals. And their success rate was typically dismal.

2. *They found themselves competing in a dynamic marketplace where the rules have changed dramatically.* Client/vendor relation-

ships have undergone a significant shift since around 1980. The contemporary business climate encourages long-term partnerships. In representing your company, you're expected to assume a broader role than that of mere vendor. Instead, you're expected to be a consultant to industry. Your career and income depend largely on your success in selling solutions—solutions that involve your products, your services, yourself.

## So . . . What's a Proposal?

Good question. Not exactly a stumper, though. Or is it?

After years of consulting in the proposal field, I'd have to say that a lot of people don't know—even those who ought to. They tend to confuse proposals with all kinds of other documents. Or they fail to understand their purpose. Or they just lose sight of the audience.

You find that hard to believe? Well, I could give you dozens of examples, but here's one that's typical. A couple of years ago I received a call from a top-level executive at one of this country's best-known industrial corporations. He said, "Some of our engineers attended a course you gave on proposal writing and said you had some different ideas. Would you like to come in to talk?"

Since I make part of my living by doing exactly that—"coming in to talk"—his invitation was certainly a welcome one. This is a company that writes proposals worth millions and millions of dollars every quarter. Its clients include governments and corporations around the globe. But its "hit rate" on proposals had been declining rapidly in recent years. The traditional proposals that managers had produced for decades no longer seemed to be doing the job. On the surface, it looked like a great opportunity. But I had some reservations.

The company in question was struggling against tough international competition and wrestling with a sagging domestic economy. But nowadays there aren't many companies that aren't facing those challenges. More disturbing was the fact that the company seemed to be struggling even harder against change. In spite of the red ink spilling across the corporate books, senior management continued to hang on tightly to old thinking, old ways of doing business, old attitudes. Would it really be receptive to new ideas?

Well, we talked, and the outcome was that I was hired to lead a two-week task force on proposals. Specifically, I was asked to help managers define a process for producing more competitive proposals and for producing them faster.

The following week, I entered a conference room to meet for the first time with a half-dozen handpicked engineers, project managers, and other professionals. After we had gotten past the appropriate introductions and niceties, I started the process by asking these professionals a question: "What's a proposal? Better yet, what's a good one?" It seemed like a harmless enough question at the time. My purpose was to make sure we all had the same thing in mind when we spoke, a common working vocabulary. I really didn't think it would create too much discomfort or consternation.

In fact, we spent the next two days wrestling with that question. What became increasingly clear was that these people—all of whom had written numerous proposals—couldn't define one. One person said, "A proposal is a technical description. It describes a system or a machine." Another suggested, "It's a document that defines the terms and conditions of our bid." A third argued that a proposal was in reality a project plan, while a fourth thought that the ideal proposal could translate directly into a contract with complete statements of terms and conditions. Pretty soon we had a free-for-all. They argued, they wrangled, they negotiated.

So who was right? Actually, none of them. After waiting a while for them to develop a workable definition of a proposal, I decided to ask a few questions: "What's the purpose of a proposal?" "Why is it worth your time and money to write proposals?" "Why do your clients request them?"

You ought to be writing proposals to sell stuff. Products, services, projects, ideas. Whatever you've got. The proposal is a marketing tool; it helps you make money by convincing people to contract with you for the kinds of things you can provide. The proposal positions your product or service as a solution to a business problem.

To do a good job, you need to make sure that your proposal is persuasive, accurate, and complete. Unfortunately, lots of proposal writers invert the order of those qualities, producing proposals that are bloated with detail and scarcely persuasive at all.

## The Value of Your Proposals to Your Clients

A good proposal can be useful both to you, the writer, and to your potential client, the recipient. How useful it is depends on how carefully it's been designed, developed, and written. If you write a good proposal, you may win more than just a specific contract. You may win good will, respect, and credibility that carry over into future business relations. Write a poor proposal and you'll almost certainly lose more than just one opportunity.

Have you ever received a proposal from somebody? If you have—and almost everybody has at least received a sales letter or two—you can probably remember how you used it. You probably formed an initial impression of the vendor and of the proposal author on the basis of the proposal's appearance and its initial accuracy: Did it spell your name correctly? Did it refer to your company correctly? Did it show any understanding of your business situation, your particular needs, the challenges you were trying to meet?

A decisionmaker may use a proposal in any combination of three basic ways:

1. To compare and screen vendors
2. To establish a base of information
3. To solicit creative solutions

▪ *Comparing and screening vendors.* Making decisions to buy products or services can be tough, especially if the decision-maker faces an array of options and has little knowledge of the particular area under consideration. In addition, many companies have sought to objectify the process of selecting a vendor, removing such subjective elements as personality from the process. Issuing an RFP allows the decisionmaker to compare and contrast responses from a variety of vendors. In fact, proposals are frequently evaluated by means of a point scale. Possessing specific areas of experience or using particular kinds of hardware may net you more points than your competitors receive because that happens to be what the evaluator is looking for. When companies hire consultants to prepare and evaluate proposals from potential vendors, the consultants often use point scales; requesting a written proposal from each candidate and evaluating the proposals objectively is one way a consultant can demonstrate that his or her recommendation is made without prejudice.

■ *Establishing a base of information.* Business puts lots of demands on decisionmakers. They need to know what's out there, who has it, and how much it costs. Issuing RFPs or just casually requesting proposals is a means of finding out what's available. I've done this myself in managing my own business. There are basic services and equipment that you may need—if not now, then eventually. By asking a potential vendor for a proposal, you can usually learn a couple of things: You can find out what's available and whether the vendor is somebody you want to work with. In my case, when the situation has been reversed and I've been asked to submit a proposal for a project or services on speculation, I'm eager to do it. Even if the client doesn't intend to buy now, providing her with accurate, insightful information in a persuasively presented package can be the beginning of a long-term relationship.

■ *Soliciting creative solutions.* What about clients who issue RFPs or request proposals from you orally with little or no intent of buying your solution? Does that happen? Yes. Is it ethical? No. If you're selling a commodity, you lose your time and effort, because you've prepared a proposal for somebody who never really intended to buy. But if you're selling a creative solution, an idea, a system design, or other intellectual property, you may have lost much more. What may happen is that the potential client will use your concept but develop it internally. Or, even more galling, that client may use your proposal as a basis for soliciting bids from your competitors. Several of my own client organizations have been burned this way. As leaders in their respective industries, they have the resources to develop elaborate system designs or to perform complex and expensive analyses in preparing a comprehensive proposal. What they've seen to their dismay is that the potential buyer has taken their proposal and used it as a requirements document, allowing competitors who can work cheaper to bid on the job. The result: Not only has effort worth tens of thousands of dollars been wasted, but the proposal writer has unwittingly set up his competitors.

To be fair to the clients, they may not know any better; they may not realize that the proposal they have received is a valuable piece of intellectual property. On the other hand, some of the people who pull these stunts will do anything they can get away with. How to protect your proprietary interests is discussed in Chapter 8.

## The Value of Your Proposals to You

Sales and marketing is a little bit like fishing. You have to figure out what kind of bait will attract the fish you want to land. You have to be patient and creative. You have to think ahead. And it helps if you put more than one hook in the water.

Think about your proposals as key sales and marketing tools, not simply as the formal means of responding to a specific request. For example, there are at least three possible ways you can use proposals as part of a comprehensive sales and marketing plan:

1. As sales documents for selling specific applications, products, or services
2. As marketing tools for creating or altering an image
3. As a means of influencing clients

▪ *Sales documents.* This is the most obvious reason to produce proposals. It probably explains why you're reading this book—to figure out how to write better proposals that will sell more. Obviously, you should write proposals that are both solicited and unsolicited, that is, proposals produced in response to RFPs or informal requests and proposals produced without any encouragement at all. Because they're more focused and show more particular knowledge of the recipient, unsolicited proposals can be more effective than direct mail at generating interest and awareness among the population of potential clients you're trying to reach.

Whenever you have a change in your pricing structure, a new service, an enhancement, a promotion, or any other blip on the screen of "business as usual," send out an unsolicited proposal to everybody who might be affected by it. You can probably use the mail merge function of your word processor to make the process quick and easy. Unsolicited proposals should be kept short and should get to the point immediately. You'll learn more about writing brief letter proposals in Section III of this book.

▪ *Marketing tools.* Think about your image. What do your clients think of you? When your company's name is mentioned, what mental images pop into their head?

Try this exercise. Take a clean sheet of paper and list the positives and negatives attached to your company. Be honest, but be fair. A typical list might look something like this:

Expensive
High-quality vendor
Reliable
Difficult to deal with/bureaucratic
Good product knowledge
Innovative
Financially stable/solid
Lots of experience
Significant local presence
Not interested in small jobs/clients

Obviously, this is a mixed list, as virtually any company's list would be. The question is how to use proposals to capitalize on the positives and to minimize or overcome the negatives. One of the negatives on the list is the fact that clients perceive your company to be expensive. Doesn't it make sense to issue an unsolicited letter proposal every time you have a price reduction, in particular identifying those current clients whose costs could be reduced by adopting the recommendation you're proposing? One of the positives on the list is that the company has a significant local presence in your market. Why not play that up in each proposal you submit? Remind the decisionmaker that he'll be dealing with a vendor who can respond to problems or concerns immediately, in person, rather than in a day or two or over the phone.

Make sure that each proposal builds on your strengths and addresses your perceived shortcomings. Even if you don't win a given bid, you may have a positive impact on the decisionmaker's assumptions about you and your company. And over the long term, that can be extremely valuable.

▪ *Influencing clients.* Good account management requires that you think about the future of your key business relationships. Merely reacting to clients' problems or needs is not nearly as effective as working with them collaboratively to develop a business direction. Each time you write a proposal, think in terms of your long-term plan for a given client. Where do you want the relationship to be in six months? In a year? In five years? What intermediate steps are necessary to get the relationship there? Perhaps you're currently providing system software to the client, but you'd also like to take on developmental projects. Begin working toward those outcomes in each proposal, looking for leverage points. If you have a choice between two or more equally legitimate solutions, recommend the one that will move the business relationship in the direction you want it to go.

In other words, start looking at proposals as your tool, your opportunity. Rather than seeing them as a kind of test that's been set up to exclude you, look at proposals as a means of accomplishing your objectives. That's the real challenge you face—not merely getting the proposal done on time, but making sure that when it's done, it accomplishes exactly what you want.

Of course, it's one thing to recognize the challenge. It's quite another to know what to do about it. That's the topic of Section II.

# Section II
# A Primer on Persuasion

# 3

# How Persuasion Happens: The "Persuasive 4-mula"

Part of the problem people have in writing proposals stems from the fact that they don't understand what persuasion is. As a result, they end up writing information. So let's begin by distinguishing among the primary reasons people write in a business setting.

When people want to present facts that other people need to do their jobs, they're writing to inform. The goal of such writing should be the economical, accurate, and easy transfer of the information. The communication fails if the reader doesn't understand the facts or, worse yet, misunderstands them.

However, sometimes people aren't trying to communicate facts alone. Instead, they're trying to interpret what those facts mean. They're offering an opinion about the significance of a certain body of information. You might compare this situation to what happens in a court case when one side calls in an expert witness. Such a witness isn't asked to establish facts about the case—"Where was the defendant on the night of July 15?" Instead, the expert witness is asked to offer an opinion about what a certain body of facts indicates. "On the basis of these facts, do you think the defendant is mentally competent?" "Given this sequence of events, did the defendant act in accord with the profession's current standard of conduct?" In the business world, each time you write a performance ap-

praisal or do a competitive analysis, you're writing an evaluation. If you merely recite the facts and don't offer your opinion,
you aren't doing the whole job.

Persuasion goes a step further. It requires presenting facts,
and it involves exercising judgment and expressing opinion.
But it also includes much more. When you write to persuade,
you're trying to influence what someone thinks, feels, or does.
You're trying to affect the audience's behavior or attitudes, or
both.

If you think about it, you're probably most comfortable
with informing. That's a writing task you feel good about.
Evaluations are probably a little tougher, and if they involve
touchy material, as a performance appraisal can, you may
dread doing them. But, for most people, the most difficult
writing task of all is persuasion. Clearly, persuasive writing
involves step-level increases in complexity and difficulty over
what the other types of communication require.

Unfortunately, when you're under pressure—particularly
if you're short of time or feel uncertain about your readiness to
proceed—you're likely to revert to the type of writing you find
easiest. For most writers, that's presenting information, usually
to an audience that's nearly as knowledgeable as the author is.
For most proposals, that's the worst possible combination of
choices—information presented at a high technical level not
only doesn't persuade, it may actually alienate the reader.

## The "Persuasive 4-mula"

For thousands of years, people have tried to figure out the best
way to persuade other people to do things. We know that
persuasion has been the subject of serious study since the days
of classical Greece. Aristotle wrote one of the great treatises on
persuasion, and among the Romans the ability to persuade
was considered a hallmark of responsible citizenship. Since
World War II, researchers have worked particularly hard to
identify the elements of persuasion. Why? They have some
practical motives: improving advertising and marketing campaigns, motivating audiences, girding consumers and voters

against propaganda, understanding the dynamics of brain-washing, and—yes—writing better proposals.

This mass of study and thought has produced little in the way of consensus. However, four basic elements have consistently emerged as a vital part of nearly every theory of persuasion. These elements apply to technical proposals, sales presentations, motivational speeches, policy statements, marriage offers, and just about every other form of persuasion encountered in modern life. So let's start there.

The four elements essential to persuasion are the *source*, the *message*, the *channel*, and the *receiver*. I call these elements the "Persuasive 4-mula," because successful persuasion requires properly mixing all four of them, like the ingredients in a chemical reaction. Each element is discussed in the following sections.

### Source

The *source* is the person or thing doing the persuading—the speaker making a speech, the sales representative trying to close a sale, the company submitting a proposal, the foundation running a public service announcement.

To be effective, the source must be both *credible* and *appealing*. Do listeners believe the source knows what he or she is talking about? Do they believe that he or she is sincere? That's the credibility issue. Do they like the person delivering the message? Do they feel comfortable with the source? Do they respect or admire the company submitting the proposal? That's the issue of appeal.

If you think about advertising, you can see how companies choose representatives on the basis of these qualities. As a spokesman for athletic shoes, Michael Jordan is both credible—he certainly knows something about sports—and appealing—he's good-looking, successful, and apparently a friendly guy. He probably wouldn't be as effective in commercials for lawn fertilizer or dump trucks. He'd still be an appealing personality, but we'd have to question the credibility of his endorsement.

Which is more important, credibility or appeal? It depends

on the audience, to some extent, and on the subject. Youngsters aren't likely to evaluate credibility very well. And something like beer or hand soap is more likely to be sold by using an appealing representative—i.e., young, fun-loving, popular, and attractive—than a credible one, such as a brewer or a chemist.

### Message

The *message* is the second element in the "Persuasive 4-mula." The impact of your message depends in part on whether the receiver is receptive to it to begin with. When the evidence or logic in a particular persuasive message is in line with the receiver's beliefs, the receiver is more likely to accept it and change his or her attitudes. If the evidence runs counter to the receiver's basic beliefs, persuasion is far less likely to occur. Thus, the way you frame your message with regard to your audience's predilections is critical.

That may seem circular: You can persuade people to accept only the things they already accept or to do the things they already want to do. But that's not quite what's going on here. There is a difference between a *belief* and an *attitude*. Someone may issue an RFP for new equipment because he or she believes that production efficiency can be improved. If you can base your proposal on the same belief and can demonstrate how you would act on it, the receiver's attitude toward *you* as the most suitable vendor will change in a positive way. However, if you send out a canned proposal, one that emphasizes the ruggedness and durability of your machines, you will not be addressing the client's basic belief. As a result, you may not persuade him or her to choose you.

### Channel

The *channel* is the medium by which your message is delivered to the receiver. Normally, your proposals will be delivered in print. But there are other options.

For example, your proposal might be accompanied by a videotape of your equipment in action. Or it might include color illustrations. Or perhaps you can deliver the actual proposal document along with a formal presentation, using overhead transparencies or slides. In those instances, you're combining audiovisual modes of delivery with the print mode. That's often a good idea, because research indicates that for relatively simple messages, an audiovisual medium is more persuasive than print alone. Recently, my own company won a large contract against much bigger competitors for extensive computer-based training and on-line documentation systems. We did it by submitting both a printed proposal and a diskette that contained an interactive graphic version of that proposal, which demonstrated our skill in developing computer-based instructional materials. It was an expensive visual aid, but it won us the job.

Remember that different receivers respond differently to the same message presented in a particular medium. A decisionmaker who likes to study information in detail and who tends to be an introvert will prefer to base decisions on a written proposal. A more intuitive decisionmaker, by contrast, would probably glance through the details in a written proposal but rely most heavily on any accompanying presentation and the overview elements.

No matter what delivery medium you use, the proposal must be persuasive. It must present clearly and convincingly the reasons your product, service, or idea can meet the client's needs or solve his or her problem. That means that you must use an underlying persuasive structure to present your material. Your proposal must *identify* the problem, state the *benefits* of solving that problem, recommend a specific *solution* to the problem, and provide the *supporting details* that allow the client to see how the solution would work. This approach is explained in more detail in Chapter 6.

### Receiver

The *receiver* is the most important component of the "Persuasive 4-mula." After all, it's the receiver who must take action, who must make a decision, or whose attitudes must change.

A message that persuades one person may leave another

one unmoved. Why? For now we can simply note that two of the factors determining how much influence persuasion has on an individual are the receiver's personality and his or her personal involvement in the issue. A person who feels threatened by change will be much harder to influence than one who feels confident and secure. Similarly, a decisionmaker will be particularly cautious in taking action on an issue that will directly affect his or her own career.

In addition, people process information in different ways. Presenting a highly detailed and analytical document to a person who prefers the "big picture" will complicate the persuasion process. Presenting information at a technical level that is too difficult for the audience to grasp will also probably doom the effort. After all, most people, when they are confused or uncertain about the information they're receiving, tend to say "No."

There are other ways to analyze the persuasive process, but this "4-mula" focuses on some of the key elements: the credibility and appeal of the source, the clarity and pertinence of the message, the effectiveness of the channel, and the preferences of the audience. Paying attention to these four keys may not guarantee success every time you try to persuade, but ignoring them almost certainly guarantees failure.

# 4

# The Source: Establishing Your Credibility

When you're trying to persuade a business manager, both credibility and appeal are necessary, but credibility is almost always more important. A decisionmaker is usually more concerned about whether you know what you're talking about than whether you talk about it in a charming way. In fact, as we mentioned earlier, that's one of the reasons businesses are using written proposals more and more frequently to select their vendors: This practice supposedly eliminates the element of appeal from the decision process. Of course, it doesn't really do that. If you turn in a sharp-looking proposal, one that's easy to read and that's written with style and grace, you're going to come across as a more appealing vendor than somebody who produces a raggedy, jargon-larded proposal. The effect may be subliminal, but that doesn't make it any less important.

In writing your proposals, ask yourself:

- *What does the decisionmaker think of me and/or my company?* The decisionmaker may have certain assumptions about you and your company that will color the review of your proposal. If you can identify those assumptions and address them, you have a better chance of appearing credible and appealing.

- *What prior experience does the client have with us?* Was it good or bad? Either way, it will influence whether you come across as credible and appealing.

- *Is the client currently using our products or services? Is it using our competitors'?* Knowledge of that experience will help you convincingly address problems and can help you tailor your presentation to capitalize on positive aspects of your previous business relationship with this client or negative aspects of the client's relationship with Brand X.

- *What must I say or do to convince the decisionmaker that I am knowledgeable, reliable, experienced, honest—in a word, credible?* We discuss this in much more detail in a few pages, because the ultimate answer to this question is: Communicate the message the way the audience wants to hear it.

- *What elements of my personality and/or my company's business philosophy will appeal to the decisionmaker?* If the decisionmaker is a no-nonsense, bottom-line kind of manager, a strictly-business approach will probably be more effective than one that focuses on the "softer" issues, such as product loyalty, employee morale, or creativity.

- *Do I understand my client's business situation and needs? Have I communicated that understanding clearly?* Credibility is usually proportional to specificity—not about your products or services, but rather about the client's business, the industry within which he or she is competing, and the operational parameters that affect your solution's operation.

- *Am I approaching my relationship with the client as a partnership?* Proposal writers often undercut their own credibility and appeal by taking too subservient a role. Their tone becomes one of supplication rather than partnership: "Thank you for allowing me the opportunity to submit my proposal and for taking time from your busy schedule to review it." Baloney! Remember that you have something important to bring to this relationship: the solution to the decisionmaker's problems or a way the decisionmaker can meet his or her needs. Be polite, of course. But don't come across as a sycophantic toady.

- *Am I offering substantive analyses of business problems based on a good understanding of my client's business functions?* If your proposal focuses on the features and benefits of your product, if it discusses size, weight, and color but never addresses why the client needs it or what it'll help the client accomplish, it's a lousy proposal. Good proposals show knowledge of the client's business, why it exists, what they're trying to accomplish, and how they go about it. That knowledge is then leveraged against what the vendor has to offer to show ways that business can be improved by adopting your recommendation.

• *Am I offering specific recommendations?* I'm amazed how often I read proposals that never contain any recommendation at all. They describe a product or service in detail; they may include management resumes, implementation schedules, and cost analyses. But they never actually recommend that the client do anything. Make a specific recommendation. Say, "I recommend that you contract with Sant and Associates for a four-week design study to determine the potential value of implementing on-line documentation in your manufacturing area." Your specific recommendation will be a call to action. It will also communicate much greater confidence and commitment.

• *Am I offering a fresh, creative solution?* Even if you're offering the same basic solution you've offered the last two dozen clients, make sure your proposal doesn't sound bored or weary. It should sound excited and enthusiastic. This is a matter of tone and attitude. Compare the difference between these two statements:

> This is a system we call a fuel regulator because it controls how much fuel enters the engine at various operating conditions.

> Your aircraft will operate even more profitably, because your engines will incorporate fuel-regulating technology—an innovative system that prevents the engine from wasting fuel at various critical points in the flight envelope.

Which one is more persuasive? Which one sounds fresh, creative? Excited?

• *Am I focusing on organizational interests rather than technical issues?* Technology in and of itself doesn't sell. Nobody buys

technology for its own sake. People buy technology because it
will have a positive impact on organizational concerns—profitability, productivity, staffing levels, quality, downtime, whatever. Focus on those issues, and show how the technology
features will deliver a big payoff in the areas that really matter
to the client.

 ▪ *Am I writing clearly, concisely, emphatically, logically, and
persuasively?* You wouldn't submit a proposal that had a coffee
stain on the title page, would you? That would undercut your
credibility and professionalism and make your offering less
appealing. Submitting a proposal that's hard to understand,
wordy, wishy-washy, illogical, or unconvicing is just as dam-
aging. Along the same lines, submitting a proposal marred by
misspellings, typos, grammar mistakes, and similar lapses also
destroys your credibility and reduces your appeal.

Your objective in writing a proposal is to provide your client
with enough information—persuasively presented information—to prove your case and motivate the client to buy your
services or applications. You must offer more than "a brochure
and a quote"—the typical proposal from those long-lost days
of yesteryear. In today's environment, every proposal should
be viewed as a competitive marketing challenge. What does
that require?

 Basically, you need to focus on four indispensable ingredients and one vital attitude. The four indispensables dictate
content; the attitude dictates commitment. And it's the attitude
that's most important.

*You must assume that the client is receiving other proposals
besides yours.* You must be as aggressive and competitive as
possible. Even if you have no evidence to the contrary, even if
you have been given every assurance by the decisionmaker that
you and you alone are the Chosen Vendor, assume that there
will be competition. In my experience, as soon as you take the
contract for granted, something bad happens. Maybe there's
some kind of pheromone associated with complacency that
decisionmakers can smell; one whiff, and they start to feel
uneasy. Next thing you know, they're saying, "Hey, why don't

we open this competition up!" Or maybe people just get sloppy when they assume it's a lock. The point is, it seems that as soon as you assume the contract's in the bag, it slips out.

Of course, that can be fun if you're on the other side of the bidding situation, competing against an entrenched vendor. I've had the opportunity to work on some proposals for clients who didn't have a chance. Everybody knew they didn't. Luckily, the competition knew it, too, and assumed it had the job won. As a result, it lost its competitive edge. And lost the contract.

As for the four indispensable elements, they're a matter of common sense. They grow naturally out of your client-centered analysis of the business case and out of your use of the persuasive paradigm (see Chapter 6) to structure your proposal. The client is reading your proposal, looking for help. For a solution. For some reassurance about the wisdom of bringing you into the picture. The client has all kinds of fears. Will they sell me the wrong thing? Will they sell me something that doesn't work? Do they really know what they're doing? Do they have enough experience? Can I trust them? If your decisionmaker works in the private sector, his or her most basic concern will be whether you will waste the company's money. If the decisionmaker works in the public sector—government or education—concern is more likely to focus on whether you will mismanage things in such a way that the project will be an embarrassment. The business owner says, "Don't waste my money." The civil servant says, "Don't make me look bad." Both are legitimate fears that your proposal should allay.

A competitive proposal must *always* include:

1. *Statements showing that you clearly understand the client's problem or need.* The reason for this one is obvious: The client's problem or need is at the heart of a client-centered persuasive proposal.

2. *A recommendation for a specific approach, program, product, system design, or application that's presented so well the client believes it will solve the problem and produce positive business results.* Simply writing in generalities about how good your stuff is won't do

the job. You need to address all of the specific elements of the statement of work or show—step by step, item by item—how your recommendation will deliver the right results.

3. *Evidence of your qualifications and competence—to deliver the solution, handle the project, or design the equipment on time, on budget, and to specification.* Reassure the decisionmaker. He or she wants to know that you can do the job, that you won't waste money or time.

4. *A convincing reason why the decisionmaker should choose your recommendation over any other's.* This is the equivalent in proposal writing of closing the sale. In a formal proposal, it appears up front, in the executive summary.

These are the essentials. Every scrap of data, every figure, every paragraph in the proposal must add something to one or more of these elements.

Why are these four essentials so important? Because they answer the decisionmaker's questions. They address the decisionmaker's fears. And they provide the decisionmaker with the key information he or she needs to evaluate your proposals successfully.

Nearly every proposal is evaluated in terms of three key factors:

1. *Responsiveness:* Do they understand my business and my current needs? Are they proposing to give me what I need, or are they proposing to sell me what they have? Worse yet, are they proposing to sell me what they'll get the biggest commission on, regardless of whether it really meets my business needs?

2. *Technical competence:* Do they know what they're talking about? Have they handled similar projects, built similar equipment, handled similar installations before? Do they have the resources to do the job? Do they have a quality control program? A change management procedure? Will their stuff work?

3. *Cost or value:* Is this a fair price? Are they hiding any costs, providing misleading cost analyses, underestimating levels of effort? What will my return on investment be if I

choose this proposal? Are there any value-added factors that make their pricing structure more appealing?

Generally the decisionmaker's evaluation is weighted in exactly that order. You may think that price is the only factor that matters most of the time. That's not true. Price is the key factor only when there's no other differentiation among proposals or when the potential client is in severe financial straits.

# 5

# The Message: Developing a Client-Centered Approach Every Time You Write

At the heart of any proposal is a solution to a problem or need. Sometimes the problem has been specified in the client's RFP; sometimes you may need to do some detective work to uncover it. Your proposal may address the problem explicitly, which is usually the best approach, or the problem may be left understood. Regardless, the important thing is that the proposal respond to that problem or need; that it be centered on the client's interests.

Unfortunately, the majority of proposals are focused anywhere but on the client's interests. A few examples:

*A manufacturer of material-handling systems had developed a standard proposal, the first twenty pages of which consisted of a history of the company. Why? It's a Fortune 500 company, so it certainly didn't need to work that hard to establish credibility. What's worse, the history was boring. It was easy to picture potential clients leafing through all that verbiage, trying to find something that addressed the RFP directly.*

*A notable research laboratory typically wrote proposals for grants that read like articles for technical journals. It plunged right in, discussing obscure technical issues, and never connected the research being proposed to the granting foundation's mission or interest. As a result, its success rate was unpredictable.*

*Account representatives for a major telecommunications vendor were constantly being pounded on the issue of price. The other guys were always cheaper—or so it was claimed. Soon the proposals from this vendor began to focus exclusively on issues of cost and value, almost completely ignoring the client's needs and the vendor's uniqueness factors. These price-paranoid proposals soon became something of a joke in the industry.*

The problem with all of these proposals was that they addressed the writers' concerns or interests long before they addressed the clients'. The proposal writers had simply failed to get out of their own heads. But very few proposals sell because they present what the writer thinks is important; they sell because they speak to the client's interests.

## Seven Key Questions

Before you ever set pencil to paper, before your fingertips ever caress a single key, answer the following seven questions. They'll force you to develop a client-centered proposal:

1. What is the client's problem or need?
2. What makes this problem worth solving? What makes this need worth addressing?
3. What goals must be served by whatever action is taken?
4. Which goals have the highest priority?
5. What products/applications/services can I offer that will achieve the desired goals?
6. What results are likely to follow from each of my possible recommendations?
7. What should I recommend?

Let's take a look at each of these questions in a little more detail, because answering them may not be as easy as it appears.

### 1. What is the client's problem or need?

Sometimes the client issues a request for proposal that specifically states what's wanted:

> The FAA needs a course to teach customer service and total quality principles to its management staff and hourly employees.

> Smith, Goldblatt, and Wong, attorneys at law, are hereby soliciting bids for an office telecommunications system to be installed in the firm's new quarters no later than May 15 of this year. The system must provide the following features: . . .

> The trustees of the Kallaher Group of Homes for the Aged solicit bids for an audit of all of the properties for the fiscal years 1990–1991 and 1991–1992.

Don't assume that the problem or need stated in the RFP is necessarily correct or complete. Read it, understand it, but keep an open mind. There may be more left unsaid that pertains to why the client is looking for help than has been included in the RFP. In addition, bear in mind that the client isn't always right. Sometimes the client thinks he or she knows what the problem is, but when you begin to look at the situation, you may find that the client is wrong. And sometimes the RFP has been patched together by a committee or has been produced by cutting and pasting old RFPs. So use the RFP as a springboard to an analysis of the business case it's indirectly presenting. It's telling you that there's a gap betwen what the issuing organization currently has or knows and what it thinks it needs in order to function effectively.

It's very likely that for some opportunities there will be no RFP. By developing your contacts with the client and by keeping your ears open, you may come across a problem or a need that you can address. That's actually a better situation for you, because you may have the opportunity to offer an unsolicited proposal without facing any direct competition.

At any rate, try to state for yourself the client's problem or need as succinctly and clearly as you can. If possible, write it out in a single sentence. (However, don't make the mistake one account executive made when she wrote to her clients, "I need to know what your problems are so that I'll know what to sell you.")

## 2. What makes this problem worth solving? What makes this need worth addressing?

Try to look behind the surface. Ask yourself why? Why now? Let's face it, there are all kinds of problems and needs out there, and most of the time we just ignore them. So what has provoked this situation now? (Usually, problems must be solved and needs must be met in a business environment when they start to have a negative impact on profitability or productivity.)

> Why does the FAA need a course on customer service and total quality principles? Why do they need it now? Why do they want to combine those two topics in the same course?

> Why is the law firm moving? How important to them is their telecommunications system? What do they include in that term? Why have they specified this group of features?

> The Kallaher Group of Homes for the Aged is insolvent. Why do the trustees need an audit now? How will they use the information? Are they looking for more than just the financial statements?

## 3. What goals must be served by whatever action is taken?

Before you can figure out what to propose, you must know what you are trying to accomplish and what you are trying to avoid.

I urge you to analyze the situation in terms of four overlapping areas: *business, technical, social,* and *personal goals.* Business goals might include such issues as capturing market share, increasing profitability, reducing overhead, creating differentiation in the marketplace, or reducing unit cost of manufacturing. Technical goals might involve automating labor-intensive processes, providing greater flexibility or modularity in system design, or enhancing quality through the use of automated machining. Social goals can be directed either internally or externally. Internal social goals might involve enhancing employee morale, increasing the professionalism of the company's representatives, or reducing turnover; external social goals might involve increasing brand recognition, changing consumer attitudes, or reducing the number of calls to a help line. Finally, personal goals include all the issues of career and prestige that the decisionmaker may be dealing with in trying to solve a problem. If the decisionmaker owns the company, there may not be as much at stake in the area of personal goals as there would be if the decisionmaker were trying to climb the corporate ladder. Note that in Figure 5-1, I have left out the circle for personal goals. That's because it can fit into the diagram any number of ways. It can stand apart from the business, technical, and social goals as an entirely separate issue in the mind of the decisionmaker; it can overlap all three goal categories; or it can be contained entirely within one of the three goal categories.

Look at all four areas. What would the ideal solution offer in each goal area? Ask yourself where these goals overlap. It's important to identify this area, because from it arises competitive leverage. This is the area where breakthrough results can be achieved. If you can provide a solution that provides positive outcomes in all four goal areas, you are increasing your client's competitiveness. Ultimately, all goals, except for the personal ones, reduce to issues of productivity and/or profit enhancement, but the more specifically you understand their impact on business functions, the more convincing your proposal will be.

### 4. Which goals have the highest priority?

You need to know what's most important to the decisionmaker. That'll tell you in what order to present your ideas when you

**Figure 5-1.** Business goal areas.

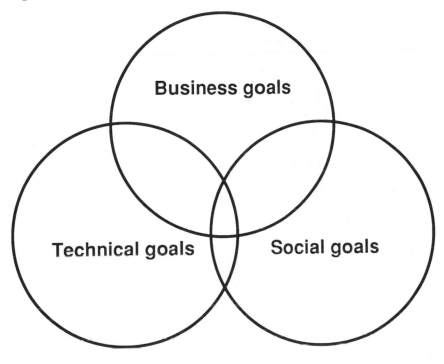

actually write the proposal. It will also help you choose among various recommendations you might make on the basis of what will deliver the best results for the client.

### 5. What products/applications/services can I offer that will achieve the desired goals?

Usually there are several ways to solve a problem or meet a need. Brainstorm. Look at all of the approaches as uncritically as possible. Consider anything. For example, you might be able to meet the needs of a client who is looking for a training program by offering a one-day seminar. Or you might be able to do it by developing a computer simulation. Or maybe you could just give the trainees a book to read, followed by a test.

The more creative you can be in combining what you know and what you have to offer, the more likely you are to separate yourself from the pack and develop a truly client-centered solution.

### 6. *What results are likely to follow from each of my possible recommendations?*

Make an educated guess about the probable results of each possible course of action. Will they lead to the client's most important goal? Will they provide competitive leverage? What will they cost? How long will they take? Are cost and timing important issues? Will they require the client to commit employees to the task?

### 7. *What should I recommend?*

Choose the best option from the client's point of view, and use that as the basis of your proposal. Even though it can be tough sometimes, try to resist the temptation to recommend the solution that offers you the highest profit margin or the biggest commission check. Manage your proposals and your business for the long term.

## Redefining the Need

Sometimes the client tells you his or her need explicitly, either through explicit definition during conversation or in the statement of work in the RFP. The trouble is, sometimes the client is wrong.

For example, suppose the manager of a telemarketing operation contacts you because she's unhappy with the sales volume her group is producing. "We need a course on closing techniques," she tells you. "Can you do that for us?"

Well, you can do it, but after observing the company's salespeople in action, you realize that what they really need is a course on telephone courtesy. Those people are rude! The question is, what do you propose?

Suppose a client issues an RFP for a computer-integrated manufacturing system, one that uses state-of-the-art technology to create a virtually unattended production facility. How-ever, in reading the statement of work, you note that the client frequently produces small batches of products and may have as many as fifteen different configurations in a typical produc-tion run. The statement of work has not addressed this factor. So what do you do?

Perhaps your CPA firm wants to bid on a major job to audit a hospital that's currently in receivership. You can do the job, but you know the hospital trustees favor one of the big firms. In addition, it's clear that a mere audit is not going to be of much help. What the hospital really needs is a full-blown analysis of Medicaid reimbursements, accounts payable, and overhead expenses, plus a plan to come out of bankruptcy. Unfortunately, the RFP has requested only a cost quote on an audit. How do you respond?

These are tough choices. You may find yourself torn be-tween wanting to propose the very best, most effective solution you can and wanting to submit the most competitive proposal possible. Clearly, if you deviate too far from what the client has requested, you may look nonresponsive. On the other hand, if you don't amend the request somewhat, you may win the job and find yourself in the uncomfortable situation of doing work you really don't think ought to be done or that you know won't deliver the desired outcomes.

The most desirable course is to communicate with the potential client, discuss your concerns or your observations, and try to educate and inform the decisionmakers before you try to persuade them. But sometimes you can't. Sometimes, when you're dealing with a formal RFP released in quantity to many potential vendors, or when you're dealing with a consul-tant who has written the RFP, or when ego or politics get in the way, you have to respond to the client's need as it's stated, even if that's not appropriate. Sometimes you have to be sensitive to the client's or the consultant's need to save face.

You have three basic options for responding to the client's stated need:

1. *Accept the need as defined in the RFP and study the various ways in which you or your company can satisfy that need, identify the*

*best among them, and propose a solution in terms of that approach.* In the short term, this is the safest approach to take. Bid on the job as it's been described, try to win it, and then hope that you can convince the client to alter the statement of work after you have the contract in your pocket. In the long term, this can be a risky approach, since you're basing the business relationship at the outset on less than full honesty.

2. *Study the business situation as accurately as you can, independent of what the proposal may tell you, and define the client's need based on your analysis.* Use your own definition of the client's need as the basis for the proposal you submit.

Redefining the need is a high-risk approach, particularly when the client has provided the original analysis or has paid a consultant to perform the analysis. Sometimes, though, you really have nothing to lose. For example, when the analysis has been provided by an outside consultant or a competitor, redefinition may be necessary in order to position your company into a more competitive relationship with the client.

3. *Do both of the above.* Respond to the client's definition of the need, but also offer an alternative perspective. You could discuss the situation frankly in the executive summary at the beginning of the proposal, stating that while you're fully prepared to respond to the statement of work as written in the original RFP, your analysis has led you to develop another approach to solving the client's problem. Or you could offer a phased approach to solving the total problem. This is a reasonably safe approach to take, particularly when the client hasn't misdefined the need but simply hasn't requested the total solution that he or she needs. By structuring your proposal in terms of phases, with each phase priced separately, you show the client what's really needed without requiring him or her to scramble the budget.

Bear in mind that redefining the need usually works only if the client can be persuaded that your redefinition is accurate. This is much easier to do if your new analysis leads toward a less costly, less time-consuming, or less complex solution. The degree of trust and credibility you and your company have established with the client is also vital. Clients are a little more likely to accept a redefinition of their computer system requirements from IBM than they are from Joe's Computer Shack.

## Developing a Consultative Proposal

Focusing on the client's need instead of your own product is the essence of taking a consultative approach. Essentially, you're trying to develop and sell a solution, not merely get an order for a commodity. As you start developing a consultative proposal—especially one that is unsolicited—you might find the following questions useful:

1. What must I establish about myself and my company before my clients will believe what I say?
2. What is the key recommendation I am making?
3. What are the specific opportunities for improving the client's productivity or profitability that I'm presenting in this proposal?
4. What are the meanings of the key words I am using? Will the client understand them?
5. To what line of reasoning is this proposal apparently a conclusion?
6. How can I contrast my proposal with other, similar proposals? (Try to anticipate how the competition may bid and—without disparaging or naming names—indicate the superiority of your approach.)
7. How inclusive (or limited) is this proposal? Should it be focused more narrowly or expanded to include more?
8. How can I illustrate or support my assertions?
9. How can I prove my claims? What kinds of evidence will the client find sufficient?
10. What can be said against my proposal? Why might somebody be opposed to it? Why might someone disbelieve it?
11. What does this proposal assume? What business objec-

tives are at its foundation? What other proposals does it take for granted?

12. Does this proposal clearly suggest that some sort of action must be taken? Does it indicate the consequences of inaction?

13. If the proposal includes a prediction or projection of results, how accurate is it likely to be? Is the prediction based on empirically observed trends, on intuition, or what?

14. What will the action called for in the proposal cost in time and money?

15. Does the proposed action involve the coordination of large numbers of people or resources? How will this coordination effort be managed?

# 6

# The Channel: Harnessing the Power of the Persuasive Paradigm

When you write to persuade, you're trying to affect how somebody thinks or feels or acts. Persuasion is tough. It's probably the most difficult and demanding communication task encountered in a business setting. More than any other form of communication, it requires you to get outside your own head and to look at things from the audience's point of view.

In the past, a proposal sometimes comprised merely a technical description of some service or application, a calculation of costs, and a calculation of payback periods. (Some companies still produce such proposals, but I have yet to see one such company that is doing very well.) Maybe those proposals worked when there was nothing else around. Today, however, the marketplace is more competitive than ever. Therefore, you need to make your proposals as persuasive as possible. You must see proposals as an integral part of your consultative role.

Remember that, rather than focusing on a service, product, or application, a persuasive proposal must focus on the client's needs. If you've followed the seven-step process outlined in Chapter 5, you're already oriented toward that kind of approach. Now the challenge is to present as persuasively as possible the information and ideas you've developed from your client-centered analysis. That means presenting your understanding of the client's business problem or need in terms that show you are deeply conscious of the client's feelings and values and making it clear that you share or respect those feelings and values.

Unfortunately, very few proposal writers know how to do that quickly and effectively. I prefer not to teach from bad examples, but sometimes it's instructive to look at how somebody has mishandled a project in order to learn from his or her mistakes. In that spirit, I present here a couple of "proposals." The first is a memo written to an internal audience; the second is a letter proposal.

## SAMPLE PROPOSAL 1

To:      Bill Henderson

From:    Woolie Crofft

Subject: Data Base Software

Today Mike Hinger stopper to explain the software available from his company which could give our executives personal access to the corporate data base in a way that would provide information to facilitate the decision-making process.

There are all kinds of things wrong with this memo, so many that it's difficult to begin to enumerate them. There's the vague subject line, the typo that transforms the verb into something that sounds like a Swedish surname ("Hinger-stopper"), the incredible sentence length, the use of nonspecific language ("personal access," "decision-making process"), and the fact that its chief organizing principle seems to be a loosely chronological stream of consciousness. But the most glaring problem, I think, is the fact that it has no clear purpose. If you were Woolie's manager, your reaction to this memo would probably be a hearty "So what?" This memo sounds like one of those worthless scraps headed "FYI," most of which end up in the garbage. It certainly doesn't look or sound persuasive. It's not addressing a problem; it doesn't clearly recommend a solution.

Sadly, the author of this memo (yes, it's an example drawn from real life, as all of these are; only the names have been changed to protect the guilty) told me how frustrated he was that "nothing had happened." "Management complains about these problems we have with the data base," he said, "but then, when you make a recommendation on how to fix it, they just ignore you." He honestly didn't perceive that his memo hadn't clearly, persuasively proposed a solution.

### SAMPLE PROPOSAL 2

March 21, 1992

Mr. Larry Barns
Director, Telecommunications Services
Information Systems Center
Challenger Automotive
P.O. Box 1476
Moreno Valley, California

Dear Larry:

It was a pleasure having dinner with you last week, and I appreciate the opportunity you gave me to present my telemarketing application.

Challenger Automotive is perceived as a leading component supplier to original equipment manufacturers of on/off highway heavy equipment, heavy duty trucks, and passenger cars and light trucks. The majority of these products are marketed to original equipment manufacturers. For this reason, Challenger product identity is usually lost to the vehicle purchaser. Advertising is aimed at equipment buyers so that when equipment purchases are made, Challenger components are specified.

In the text of the advertisement, Challenger encourages the consumer to write in for further information concerning the product. In some instances, a catalog which is published periodically listing the name, telephone number, and address of dealers and distributors who stock Challenger components is mailed to the consumer.

The risk inherent in this method of advertising involves consumers contacting distributors who no longer carry Challenger components or who are simply out of stock. On the low end of the risk scale, the distributor will refer the buyer to another distributor. This lengthens the buying cycle. On the high end, the distributor will sell the buyer a similar component supplied by a manufacturer other than Challenger.

The solution to this problem is telemarketing, specifically a product we refer to as "Dealer On-Line." Here is a brief description of how it works: The advertisement for the component will carry an 800 number. The consumer will call in on this number and reach a Challenger representative for the After-Market Sales Group. Using an electronic data base, the representative can direct the consumer to the nearest distributor of Challenger components.

Considering your initial response to my presentation of this concept, I know we have a solid application with "Dealer On-Line," and I am looking forward to presenting it to the Sales and Marketing group at the division with your support.

Sincerely,


André LeToille


This letter is truly awful. It starts with a hackneyed sentence that's both inappropriate and weak. It's inappropriate because it implies that the salesperson was allowed to deliver his ideas only because he bought the client dinner. And it's weak because the tone is not one of partnership, but rather of subservience: "Thank you for letting me present . . ."

Then the letter wastes the client's time telling him what kind of business he's in. That's helpful! Is the client supposed to deduce from this information that the salesperson understands him thoroughly?

It's not until the fourth paragraph that there is anything substantive—a hint of a business problem, namely, that the advertising is probably not as effective as it could be. But the solution sounds so canned that the reader begins to suspect that perhaps the salesperson was somebody with a product in search of a need.

Finally, the ending is even weaker than the beginning. The writer completely abdicates responsibility for the selling process and doesn't really ask for anything. Certainly not for a sale.

Both of these sample proposals suffer from the same weakness. They're not organized in a way that clearly, effectively, *persuasively* communicates to the audience. In other words, they're not broadcasting their messages over a channel that's being picked up by the receiver's headset.

And there is such a channel. I call it the persuasive paradigm.

## The Persuasive Paradigm

It's a simple fact that you will do a better job of writing if you know what you're trying to accomplish: the *why* of a given document. And knowing the why will help you figure out the *how*: the appropriate format or structure. Each of the three purposes for which people write in an organizational environment—information, evaluation, and persuasion—has its own unique pattern, its own paradigm.

Fortunately, the persuasive paradigm is pretty simple:

- Establish the *need* or *problem* being addressed, one that the reader/decisionmaker will recognize as genuine and accurate.
- Point out the *benefits* of solving that problem or meeting that need. There are lots of problems. Why is it worthwhile to solve this one? What's the probable return on investment? Don't confuse benefits with product features. Instead, focus on organizational or personal improvements, especially in the Two Ps: Productivity and Profitability. Even if the need or problem has been iden-

tified in the client's RFP, it's still a good idea to spell out your understanding of the payoff to be expected from solving the problem. That will help establish common goals and measurable objectives, two requirements for a partnership.

- Recommend the *solution*. Be sure to make a firm, clear recommendation: "We recommend the immediate installation of ASAP mainframe software." Don't be wishy-washy. Don't depend on telepathy to get your point across.

- Provide the *supporting details* the reader needs to understand your solution technically, to see that you are a credible, reliable provider of such solutions, and to understand the cost issues, particularly return on investment.

These four elements are described in Figure 6-1.

**Figure 6-1.** The persuasive paradigm.

---

| NEED/PROBLEM: | Catch the reader's attention by stating a specific need or problem that he or she has. |
|---|---|
| BENEFITS: | Spell out clearly the payoff from meeting the need or solving the problem, and the possible consequences of inaction. |
| SOLUTION: | Discuss specifically what you want the reader and his or her company to do. Answer the most commonly asked questions:<br>   &bull; Why should we do this now?<br><br>   &bull; Why are the obvious alternatives not as good as this solution?<br><br>Make a specific recommendation accompanied by action steps. |
| SUPPORT: | Discuss related issues, cost details, management issues, schedules, risks, future implications, but most importantly return to your key selling point—the recommendation presented in terms of a quantified cost/benefit ratio. |

---

Lots of really bad proposals begin with the history of the bidding company or with a technical description of the solution. These proposals don't work because they don't address the key factor that will motivate the reader to decide to buy: a perception of need, the gap that exists between what is and what ought to be, particularly one that offers a big payoff once the need is met.

If we revisit the bad examples we examined at the start of this chapter and apply the persuasive paradigm to them, we see some dramatic changes.

## REVISED SAMPLE 1

To:       Bill Henderson

From:    Woolie Crofft

Subject: Increasing Executive Access to the Data Base

Our executives need access to the corporate data base. The information it contains will be invaluable in helping them develop strategies, make decisions, and respond quickly to changing marketing conditions. Unfortunately, they are currently blocked from obtaining that information by a number of system-related problems.

Software available from Hinger Associates will remedy the situation. It interfaces easily with our existing system, creating a user-friendly "shell" that allows each person to select, format, and manipulate the data he or she needs without affecting the data base itself. I recommend that we lease this software system for a six-month trial with an option to buy.

Mike Hinger, the developer of the system, indicated that installation would take about four days. He will provide all the necessary documentation and support. A six-month lease runs $2,500, with the full amount credited toward the purchase price of $5,800. If it offers even a modest increase in executive productivity, it will pay for itself well before the trial period is through.

Shall we proceed?

## REVISED SAMPLE 2

March 21, 1992

Mr. Larry Barns
Director, Telecommunications Services
Information Systems Center
Challenger Automotive
P.O. Box 1476
Moreno Valley, California

Dear Mr. Barns:

As you mentioned during our meeting on Tuesday, these are extremely competitive times in the automotive industry. In such an environment, can Challenger Automotive afford to advertise for its competitors?

Obviously not. Nobody can. And yet that may be what's happening each time Challenger runs an ad aimed at the consumer segment of the market without including an 800 number that can connect consumers immediately with up-to-date information about the location of their nearest Challenger dealer.

The current advertisement encourages consumers to write in for information about the product and for a catalog that lists the names, telephone numbers, and addresses of dealers who stock Challenger components. But consumers want convenience. They don't want to wait. And even if they are willing to wait, there's no guarantee that the catalog will be current. The dealer might be out of stock or may no longer carry Challenger components. The net result would be your advertising resulting in a sale for your competitors.

I recommend the installation of an 800 number—1-800-CHAL-LENGE. When a potential customer calls in on this number, a Challenger representative from the After-Market Sales Group will use an electronic data base to direct the caller to the nearest distributor of Challenger components.

Challenger's advertising campaign is a winner. With the addition of a customer-focused tool like the CHALLENGE number, it can yield breakthrough performance. Attached are brief descriptions of the results a similar system delivered for other companies and a pricing summary. We can install the system and have it fully functional within six weeks of your go-ahead. And sales can begin to soar immediately thereafter!

Sincerely,


André LeToille

# 7

# The Receiver: Using the Cicero Principle to Reach the Audience

The essence of client-based persuasion can be summarized in the words of the Roman orator and statesman Cicero:

> "If you wish to persuade me, you must think my thoughts, feel my feelings, and speak my words."

This is great advice, so excellent that it is the basis for this entire chapter. When we break it down, phrase by phrase, we can see just how profound it is.

### *If you wish to persuade me . . .*

Why do you wish to persuade anybody of anything? Basically, you're hoping to influence their behavior, thinking, or attitude. If the context of the persuasion is sales, you're trying to motivate the audience to purchase your product or service. If the context is training, you're trying to motivate the audience to use certain techniques or procedures on the job. If the context is politics, you may be trying to win a vote.

Simply put, the purpose of persuasion is to influence how somebody acts. As the English philosopher John Locke pointed out, human nature being what it is, people usually act in their own self-interest. Clearly, then, in structuring a proposal to be as persuasive as possible, to lead the client to say "Yes!" to your recommendation, you must position it so that it's clearly in the client's own best interest.

### . . . *you must* . . .

Old Cicero doesn't cut us any slack here. This is mandatory. Not "it would be a good idea if" or "beneficial results may derive from." Nope. *You must.* And he's right, because what he goes on to discuss is the necessity of developing your persuasive arguments from the client's perspective.

### . . . *think my thoughts* . . .

One of the keys to thinking like the client is to try to see things from his or her point of view. In fact, that may be the fundamental key to all persuasion: getting outside your own head and away from your own interests and trying to get inside the decisionmaker's head.

To think the thoughts of your audience, you need to look at his or her role in the decision-making process. Is the decisionmaker also a hands-on user of your product or service? That person is probably most concerned with the reliability, user friendliness, and productivity of what you're offering and its compatibility with existing systems or equipment. Is the decisionmaker a gatekeeper who is primarily concerned with a narrow range of issues? That person is thinking about technical factors, such as engineering specifications, legal requirements, or contractual obligations. Or is the decisionmaker the ultimate authority, the one who controls the checkbook, the one who says yes or no? Chances are that person is looking at bottom-line issues of cost, productivity, return on investment, and other measures of business performance.

### . . . *feel my feelings* . . .

Factors that trigger a strong, positive emotional response in one person may produce no response at all in another. To persuade somebody, you must pay attention to what counts the most in that person's world view. That way you can get a sense of the person's basic personality style, orientation to the world, and preferred mode of dealing with information.

### . . . and speak my words.

The last element is absolutely vital. Most of the time, you should use words you're confident the audience will understand. And if there's a discrepancy between the language your audience uses and what you use, you should drop your own usage and mimic the audience. Your readers will understand more, feel more comfortable with the proposal, and be more likely to adopt your recommendation.

In my experience as a consultant, no matter what the company is selling—whether it be a product or service, high tech or low—these Ciceronian principles of client-based persuasion work.

## Analyzing the Audience

Cicero has given us the word: You must consider your audience when writing proposals. It's crucial. Ignoring or misunderstanding the audience dooms hundreds of proposals to failure every year, proposals that otherwise answer the needs or solve the problems of the corporations soliciting them.

The problem is that most people write proposals under duress. They don't want to do it. They don't have enough time to do it. And they don't feel fully qualified to do it. So they grab something off the shelf at the last minute, switch around the client names (hoping they haven't missed one somewhere!), and send it out. Who is that proposal designed to reach? Certainly not the people who will be getting it!

Or they hastily write an original proposal but ignore the audience. Instead, they write what they'd like to get. If they're technical and detail-oriented, their proposals reflect that orientation. If they're focused on bottom-line issues, that's how they write. How likely is it that the client will have the same attitudes and personality traits you have? And even if he or she does, how likely is it that he or she will be comfortable with the same language you are?

As Cicero has indicated, then, to write a winning proposal, you need to consider three key factors about the audience:

1. Personality type
   - Detail-oriented
   - Pragmatic
   - Consensus-oriented
   - Visionary
2. Technical level
   - Expert
   - Informed
   - Initiated
   - Uninitiated
3. Operational role
   - Ultimate authority
   - User
   - Gatekeeper

To appeal to and hold the interest of this broad spectrum of readers, you must balance many presentation skills, providing enough technical data to please the highly informed, detail-oriented readers, but not so much that the visionaries will be bored or the lay audience intimidated.

## The "You" Attitude

For years, experts in business writing have urged their clients to write with a "you" attitude. Usually this meant focusing on the audience, the reader, rather than on themselves, making the tone personal, warm, and friendly, and making it speak to the reader as directly as possible. Sometimes the advice has been very literal: Writers were urged to use the pronoun *you* and avoid any use of *I*.

Writing with a "you" attitude is good advice as long as it's tempered with some common sense and insight. First of all, simply using the word *you* does not automatically orient a communication toward the reader. For example:

Dear Jack:

You've probably wondered why your investment portfolio has performed so miserably this quarter. As you know, your stocks have failed to meet expectations, and you've actually trailed the market's growth and the rate of inflation. But you'll probably be a little surprised, my friend, to find out how bad it's really been. The fact is, you're broke.

There is not an *I* to be found anywhere and lots of *you*'s, but this letter is no model of empathy.

So if the "you" attitude isn't achieved simply by using that particular pronoun, how is it achieved?

The short, simple answer is that you have to try to get into the reader's mind. We all wear a pair of glasses and a pair of hearing aids that filter what we see and hear so that reality remains in harmony with our assumptions. Taking off our glasses, pulling out our hearing aids, can be extremely difficult.

## Adjusting to Different Personality Types

The first factor about your reader that you need to assess is personality type. There are many tools available for analyzing and categorizing personalities. One of the most useful I've encountered for analyzing and understanding decisionmakers is the Myers-Briggs [Personality] Type Indicator, used by career counselors, family and marital therapists, educators, and many others to help people understand themselves and others better.

The Myers-Briggs Type Indicator (MBTI) evaluates an individual's preferences among four pairs of opposing personality preferences: introversion/extraversion; sensing/intuitive; thinking/feeling; and judging/perceiving. The first pair has to do with the way people prefer to interact with the world. The second pair indicates the two general ways people prefer to gather data. Some people, for example, are by nature oriented toward facts and tend to be very literal in their use of words; they need to look at all the details before reaching a conclusion. These people, in the MBTI terminology, are "sensors." Their opposites, the "intuitives," find details boring and distracting. They prefer the big picture and appreciate the value of the generalist in an organization. The third pairing, the thinking/feeling dichotomy, focuses on how people prefer to make decisions. Thinkers look at issues objectively, reach conclusions based on what's fair and logical rather than on what makes people happy, and find logic and technical detail more credible and appealing than emotion. Feelers, by contrast, consider a good decision to be one that builds consensus and harmony. They often make decisions by asking how any given course of action will affect the people involved, and they consider service and quality to be as important as profit. The final pairing, judging/perceiving, indicates a person's preferred way to organize his or her time. Judgers prefer punctuality, structure, order, and closure. Perceivers prefer to "go with the flow." Spontaneity and flexibility are more important to them than organization.

This brief summary of the Myers-Briggs approach does a disservice to a subtle, nonjudgmental, and extremely rich method of discussing personalities. By combining these various traits, it's possible to define sixteen different "types" of personality. Sixteen types is a bit unwieldly, however, and it's pretty difficult to get your audience to take the Myers-Briggs test and let you evaluate the results. You really don't need a detailed, clinical picture of the decisionmaker, though. The kind of information you need is the kind you can garner from commonsense observation. What is the person's manner of speaking? Curt? Detailed? Emotional? Look at his or her office. How is it decorated? Are there schematics of jet engines on the wall or pictures of the kids? Are there golf and tennis trophies or Sierra Club posters? What really seems to matter to this person? In my proposal writing seminars I ask participants to quickly write down "ten things I love." They only get a couple of minutes to do it, so their answers have to be spontaneous.

What they say they love is often a clue to what kind of personality type they are. Then I ask them, "Could you fill out a list of the ten things your key client loves? If not, start paying attention. Learn about the decisionmaker as a person so that you know what kind of person he or she may be."

The crucial personality characteristics that you need to consider when looking at your decisionmakers are how they prefer to gather data and how they prefer to make decisions. I suggest that you set up a matrix based on those variables and position your key decisionmakers as accurately as possible within it (see Figure 7-1). Understanding the intended audi-

**Figure 7-1.** Ways of gathering data and making decisions.

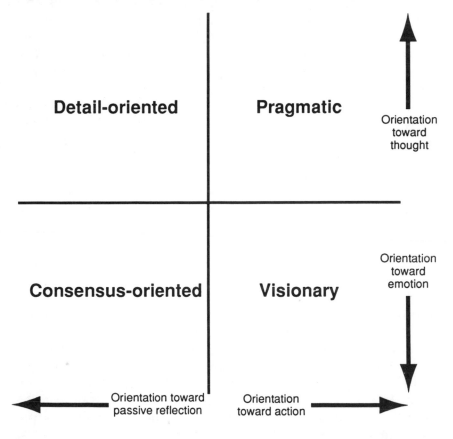

ence's orientations can help you structure your persuasion so that its appeal is as powerful as possible.

*Detail-oriented* decisionmakers approach experience rationally and logically. They tend to dislike emotional terms and inexact language. They often want lots of detail and substantiation before they accept a new idea. For them, truth occurs as facts, formulas, or procedures. They constantly evalute a presentation or document, even while perceiving it. They're likely to accept length and detail if they support the points being made. Words that may trigger a quick, strong response in an analytical reader include *experience, factual, proven,* and *principles.*

*Pragmatic* types are results-oriented, bottom-line-oriented. They want action. They tend to ask, "How can I use this now? What's the point? What's in this for me?" They are strongly oriented toward the bottom line and want it presented quickly. As a result, they may be impatient, especially with lengthy or detailed material. They appreciate straightforward logic and documents or presentations that are precisely organized and that stay on track. You might trigger a strong, positive response from a pragmatic by using words and phrases such as *planned, completed, mission, objective, return on investment,* and *competitive advantage* in presenting your message.

*Consensus* types sincerely want to understand and to feel certain that everyone involved in a decision is comfortable with it. They're open to you as a writer and to your message. They may have flashes of insight into you as an individual and into your meaning. They're also likely to pick up inconsistencies between your apparent message and your hidden intentions. They're inclined to make erroneous assumptions, garble technical data, or introduce unwanted emotional messages. Trigger words for consensus builders may include *consensus, flexible, adaptable, reliable,* and *dependable.*

*Visionaries* are people who manage their lives, their responsibilities, and others on the basis of instinct and intuition. They're the opposite of detail-oriented, in that they leap over logic and facts in quest of action. They're easily bored with technical data and love to be involved. On the down side, they have a hard time hearing any message that upsets their feelings or challenges their assumptions or biases. Visionary trigger words include *hunches, possible, innovative, ingenious,* and *creative.*

These characteristics are summarized in Figure 7-2.

Sometimes people's job responsibilities require them to act like a certain type of person even when that's not their true type. A high-level manager almost has to think "pragmatically," and a person with technical responsibilities may have to adopt an "analytical" approach. Should you write to the "real" person or the "role" person? I think that depends on whether you're trying to inform or persuade. Information will be most acceptable if it's structured for the role; persuasion will be most successful if it's pitched to appeal to the real.

## Adjusting for Different Technical Levels

As you write your proposal, you must pay attention to the level of technical expertise your reader possesses. If you don't consciously slant what you write toward a specific audience, you'll probably end up writing to yourself; you'll use the words and make the assumptions that you're comfortable with. But how many readers are there who know as much as you do about your topic? How many of them use the same words, understand the jargon, can recognize the acronyms as something other than alphabet soup?

Writers who know their reader thoroughly, who know that reader's background and level of knowledge, produce more effective work. Professional writers have to slant everything they write, to meet the style and expectations of a given magazine, editor, or readership. As a writer of business or technical proposals, you also need to understand how to slant what you write.

One of the most important differences among readers is their level of expertise. How much does a particular reader know about the subject you're discussing? How easily will he or she understand the technical aspects of the proposal? Generally, people overestimate what others know about their area

**Figure 7-2.** A summary of personality types.

**Detail-oriented:**
- Constantly evaluates the presentation.

- Edits the information and prepares a response while reading or listening.

- Dislikes emotional terms, inexact language.

- Ignores or fails to understand elements of the subtext.


**Pragmatic:**
- Results-oriented. Wants action.

- Asks, "How can I use this now? What's the point?" Wants the bottom line presented quickly.

- Tends to be impatient.

- Analyzes both the text and the subtext, trying to separate emotion from logic.

- Appreciates straightforward logic, presentations that are precise and that stay on track.

**Consensus-oriented:**
- Sincerely wants to understand. Open to the writer and the message.

- Has flashes of insight into the writer's self and meaning. Picks up inconsistencies between the message and the intention of the writer.

- Inclined to make erroneous assumptions, garble technical data, or introduce unwanted emotional messages.

**Visionary:**
- May have difficulty in seeing the proposal writer as a partner, but once "converted" becomes a true champion.

- Can't hear any message that upsets feelings or challenges his or her assumptions/biases. Prone to "Not Invented Here" attitudes.

- Leaps over logic and detail in quest of action.

- Likes to be involved. Easily bored with technical data.

of interest. They take their own knowledge for granted and therefore assume that others share their level of expertise.

Levels of expertise vary along a continuum, but I've found it convenient to think in terms of four levels of readership. This allows enough discrimination among readers to significantly alter your writing style but is not unwieldy. Of these four levels, you're likely to encounter only three when you write proposals. The fourth level, the expert, is extremely rare.

### The Uninitiated Audience

Uninitiated readers have virtually no background in your subject. They may be very bright and well-educated in some areas, but not in yours. (We're all at this level sometimes. As Will Rogers once said, "Everybody's ignorant, just on different stuff.") Even if you are dealing with government agencies or industry giants who should know all about the products or services you provide, you'll find that they're populated with lay audiences—new hires, specialists in other areas, or people whose responsibilities are so general that they no longer keep track of all the technical details. The CEO, to cite a fairly typical example, may have been an engineer at one point in his or her career, but today that person's responsibilities are unlikely to include nuts-and-bolts technical detail. As a result, the CEO may now be nearly as uninformed as a lay audience.

Here are some guidelines to help you slant your writing toward lay audiences:

1. *Provide only the information the reader truly needs to know.* Avoid digressions into technical details or options, no matter how interesting they may be to you.
2. *Keep the presentation basic.* Short is better than long. Functional value is a better focus than operational complexity.
3. *Use clear, graphic illustrations generously.* Think in terms of both visual illustrations (photos, simple charts and graphs, trend curves) and verbal ones (descriptions, comparisons, case studies, analogies, examples).
4. *Avoid any use of jargon and keep acronyms to a minimum.*

Don't forget that for these readers, product names are jargon. Don't assume that they will recognize your product and know exactly what it does.

5. *Keep both the words and the sentences simple and short.* Use words of one and two syllables mainly. Try to keep your sentences to an average length of seventeen to twenty words. In writing simply, you're not necessarily writing simplistically. By presenting information clearly, you're not guilty of patronizing the reader.

6. *Avoid references to specialized reports, manuals, or sources.* This level of reader won't look for them, wouldn't understand them, and probably doesn't care.

7. *Present procedures in step-by-step fashion.* Simple chronological structures work better than a sequence of complex options. Use flow charts whenever possible.

8. *Use a maximum of highlighting techniques to clarify the key points, to make structure visible, and to reinforce the message.* Boldface type, headings, bullet points, underlining, color—use anything that makes your key points jump off the page.

### The Initiated Audience

An initiated audience may have considerable education or experience, perhaps even in your general area (business management, electrical engineering, marketing, accounting, whatever), but has no detailed knowledge of your specific field. Many of the decisionmakers to whom you write proposals will be at this level.

All of the preceding guidelines are appropriate for the initiated audience. You won't offend them by being too easy to understand. However, you can make more assumptions and skip over the basics a little quicker.

Here are some guidelines to follow:

1. *Provide an overview—a frame of reference within which the reader can place your proposal.* This can be a discussion of the client's business objectives, operational concerns,

or a key policy. Often you can use it as the springboard for your discussion of the problem.
2. *Use more complex graphics, tables, and figures.* However, you should still avoid equations, programming statements, schematics, decision trees, and other specialized illustrations. Resist the urge to photocopy illustrations from technical manuals.
3. *Include more technical reports, surveys, documentation, brochures, manuals, and so forth, if necessary.* However, put this stuff in the appendix, and challenge it before you use it. Will it really help?
4. *Use accepted terminology of the general field, but avoid in-house jargon.* When in doubt, don't use the jargon. It's better to be too clear than too difficult.

### The Informed Audience

This audience has extensive knowledge of your field but little knowledge of the specialized project or services you are proposing. For example, a long-time client may not know much about your other product lines.
Some guidelines:

1. Establish immediate links between the familiar and the new.
2. Focus on the uniqueness factors or on the parts of the product, service, or offering that the audience doesn't know.
3. Remember, even though this audience is more familiar with your technology, jargon, and procedures, you must still write a client-centered proposal, one that addresses the client's problems or needs from the organizational (not the technical) point of view.

### The Expert Audience

The expert audience possesses extensive knowledge of your specialized product, project, or services and has detailed familiarity with the latest work in the field. In reality, there are very few people inside organizations who fit this description, much less people on the outside among your clients. That's probably lucky for you, since if there were lots of people who knew all about your responsibilities, your organization wouldn't need you anymore, would it?

Here are some guidelines for writing for this group:

1. Provide technical background information or indicate where it can be obtained.
2. Use jargon (judiciously) and provide references.
3. Maintain your objectivity and a professional tone.
4. Use math and/or technical explanations freely if they're needed.

These guidelines can help you communicate more effectively, but first you have to understand thoroughly your reader's point of view. Remember: Most people overestimate how much others know. When in doubt, simplify

## The Organizational Role of the Decisionmaker

The third element about your reader that you must evaluate as you prepare your proposal is the reader's role in his or her organization. Ideally, every proposal you write will go directly to the hands of the final authority, the one person charged with responsibility for issuing the purchase order or signing the contract. But in this imperfect world of ours, you may have to deal with intermediary decisionmakers, winning their approval before you get to the final throne of power. Understanding how the concerns of the decisionmaker change depending on his or her role can help you position your proposal as effectively as possible.

### The Gatekeeper

A person who has the role of gatekeeper is there to winnow the number of proposals down to a manageable few. The gatekeeper's role is to filter out solutions that are inappropriate in terms of some set of technical specifications. As a result, the gatekeeper is usually looking for reasons to reject rather than reasons to recommend you. In addition, gatekeepers may often feel that they're in a vulnerable position, since their recommendation could come back to haunt them if it proves to be a bad one. Their tendency, therefore, is to be extremely critical and to assume the worst whenever they have doubts. Finally, gatekeepers are often drawn from that category of people who love details. As a result, you must provide the gatekeeper with clear, specific evidence that you meet the requirements of the RFP.

### The User

The user bases his or her recommendation on less specific, technical criteria than those used by the gatekeeper. The user evaluates the probable impact of your solution on performance: Will this work? Will it actually help us? Is it user-friendly? Is it easy to maintain? Does it meet our needs?

The user has a lot of power, sometimes much more than the gatekeeper, because the user will end up actually using the product or service. And the user knows that lots of solutions that meet the technical specs established in an RFP don't actually do the job when they're installed.

### The Ultimate Authority

The person who makes the final decision, who has veto power over the project, usually derives his or her power from direct access to or control over the money. The ultimate authority is the boss, the owner, the CEO. And the ultimate authority's criteria are the needs of the business. What will be the bottom-line impact of this solution? What kind of return will this investment provide?

### Evaluate Your Evaluators

In the case of big-dollar RFPs, as many as 70 percent of all proposals are evaluated by consultants. For smaller purchases and RFPs issued by medium-size companies, the evaluator is more likely to be a responsible manager within the client organization's own staff. Sometimes the client assembles a committee of evaluators to review the proposal. The evaluation committee's members may be experts in certain functional areas of the company and yet not be familiar with the product or service they're buying. In fact, they may not see the whole proposal; they may be given sections to evaluate independently.

Make every effort to determine exactly how your proposal will be evaluated. Find out as much as you can about the evaluators, their areas of expertise, their normal jobs. What kinds of personalities do they have? Who are the dominant members of the evaluation team?

What should you do about the issue of personality type when you're dealing with a committee of evaluators? Won't there be a mixture of all kinds of personalities? Yes, there will. But think about what happens in the meetings you attend, in the committees on which you've served. Normally, the group has a nominal leader who has been appointed to that position. But as it begins to function, the pragmatic personalities take over, driving the group toward decisions and closure. They're tempered to some extent by the analytical types, who want "evidence" before final decisions are made. However, the other types tend to be ignored or run over. Therefore, when writing a proposal that will be evaluated by a committee, assume a pragmatic personality and structure the proposal to be direct and bottom-line-oriented. Then, assume a secondary personality orientation toward details and analysis, which you can satisfy by putting the facts in a subordinate section behind an overview.

What about consultants? Usually they play the gatekeeper role. If the consultant is an expert in a particular industry or technology, you can assume that the criteria by which he or she will screen proposals will be technical. On the other hand, if the consultant is from a major accounting firm, the criteria may be skewed more toward cost, return on investment, and project control issues.

Here are some questions to ask as you begin developing

your proposal. The answers will help you successfully evaluate your evaluators:

1. What issues are important to the evaluators as a group? as individuals?
2. What is their perception of my company? my products or services?
3. What biases do they have concerning my company, and how will these biases affect the scoring of my proposal?
4. Does another vendor have a preferred position with the evaluators?
5. How much do the evaluators know about our proposed solution, and how much additional information will they need?
6. What will the evaluators be looking for when they evaluate our response?
7. How much weight will they give technical merit? cost? maintenance and support? project management?

## Tips for Writing Proposals

Try to think like the reader as you write your proposal. Write to your reader's level, not to your own or that of your technical peers.

Here are some tips:

- Make it easy for the evaluators to find out why they should prefer your company to any of your competitors. Make the information easy to find, and make your compliance with the RFP obvious and easy to understand. A compliance matrix is a good idea for this purpose. List each requirement from the RFP's statment of work. Then indicate whether you will meet that requirement in full, with modifications, or not at all. However, don't let the compliance matrix stand alone in providing information to the evaluators about your offering. Back it up with discussion sections, and in particular address any areas where your compliance is partial or incomplete.

- Use simple, direct language. Use the language that appears in the RFP. If the RFP calls for a plan, give them a plan.

- Avoid a patronizing tone, but don't make too many assumptions about what the evaluators already know. Don't omit information because you think they already know it or because they should know it. This is particularly true if you're dealing with consultants. They may use only the information contained in the proposal to make their judgments, regardless of what common sense or common knowledge may tell them.

- Never assume you have an edge because of a personal relationship with the decisionmaker or because of private hints or suggestions. Write competitively.

- Don't rewrite the RFP requirements, and don't imply that a particular requirement is foolish, inappropriate, unnecessary, unsophisticated, technically backwards, or unworkable. Even if it is.

- Don't attack competitors by name. Instead, merely point out the weaknesses in particular solutions or approaches without mentioning by name the likely source of such approaches.

- Sell your solution, but don't get carried away into offering hype, fluff, or exaggeration. Remember: The proposal is a legal document, and when you win, it becomes part of the contract.

- Do justify and support your claims with specifics, quantifying whenever possible. Evaluators tend to be harsh with vendors who simply promise to comply with a requirement. They look favorably upon vendors who tell them how they'll meet the requirement.

# Section III

# How to Manage the Process and Keep Your Sanity

# 8

# An Overview of the Proposal Development Process

One of my clients recently shared an embarrassing story during a seminar. It seems that after working on a proposal for several weeks, she found herself, accompanied by her secretary, in the back seat of a cab, racing across town, shuffling papers, desperately trying to assemble three copies of a proposal, in hopes of beating a 3 P.M. deadline. Along the way, their frantic efforts so distracted the cab driver that he ended up hitting another car. At that point, my client grabbed her papers and began running, in high heels, toward the client's headquarters. She got there too late and blew the deal.

Clearly, something has gone dreadfully amiss if this is the way any project ends up. Unfortunately, this story is all too typical. Managing a proposal can become a real nightmare. It can challenge your sanity. At the end you may feel you've gained new insight into the concept of a Pyrrhic victory. It doesn't have to be that way, of course. This chapter addresses some of the key issues involved in managing a proposal project and in assembling the team that puts it together.

If you're self-employed, or if you're a one-person marketing department, you may look at the notion of a team with wistful longing. For you, there is no team, and the project is totally under your control. However, even when you're working alone, an understanding of the steps in the proposal development process can be helpful to you.

Basically, the flow of activities involved in developing your proposal should look something like Figure 8-1.

## Make Preproposal Decisions

Basically there are two decisions that you must make before you begin any work on the proposal itself:

- Is this job worth bidding on?
- How much effort should I put into the proposal?

### Perform a Bid/No Bid Analysis

Good proposals are expensive. They're time-consuming. They can soak up valuable resources. Is it really worth it to make that kind of investment in hopes of winning the potential business being offered in this RFP?

In my experience, too many companies quote on jobs that they really don't want to win. Let's face it, not all business is business that's worth having, and there's no point in wasting time and resources putting together a strong proposal for a contract you'd regret winning. In addition, there are opportunities out there that you'd love to have but that you're really not in the running for. Perhaps the client requires experience, resources, technology, or logistical capabilities that you just don't have. In proposal writing, optimism is vital; wishful thinking is a waste. Use a bid/no bid analysis to limit the quoting you do to opportunities that are most likely to result in an order. In fact, smart companies establish a review board to control which RFPs or other opportunities become active. This selectivity results in only high-probability quotes entering the system.

The bid/no bid analysis should be flexible and varies from company to company and industry to industry. I urge you to develop your own bid/no bid analysis scheme. Some of the issues that you might want to consider include:

- Is this project or acquisition funded?
- If not, are funds available within the client's budget?

**Figure 8-1.** Flow chart for development of a proposal.

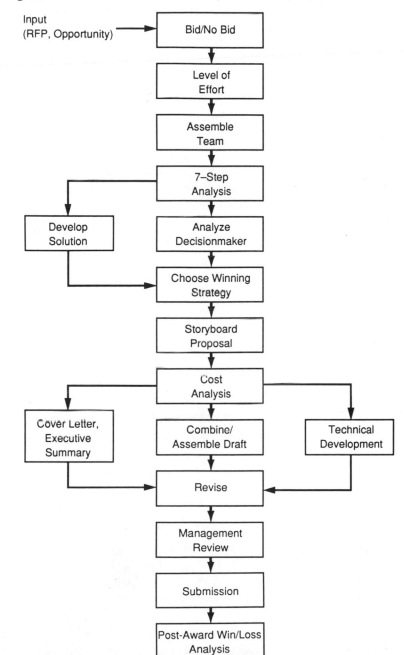

- Is the client serious about the RFP or is it just exploring?
- Will writing this proposal involve large amounts of R&D work?
- Will it require heavy investments of time and money to complete?
- Would winning this competition further your company's own goals? Is it good business?
- Are there strong political considerations regarding this bid?

If you decide to "no bid" an RFP, ask yourself what consequences that action may have downstream. Will a "no bid" decision limit future opportunities to bid on this customer's business? If a consultant is involved, will a "no bid" decision affect your company's relationship with that consultant in the future?

If you do decide not to go forward, notify the customer promptly of your decision. Explain in specific terms why you have decided not to bid on the job. Make clear which requirements or issues pose a difficulty, and indicate that you remain interested in meeting the customer's future needs.

### *Determine the Level of Effort*

The second preproposal decision that you need to make is how much effort to put into the proposal. Establishing some general guidelines to help determine the amount of effort to put into preparing a proposal makes this decision easier. Some criteria to consider:

- Immediate and long-term value of the proposal
- Potential profitability of the proposal
- Long-term potential to establish a preferred-vendor relationship with this client
- Potential to gain competitive advantage by winning the competition

You may choose to categorize the level of effort as follows:

A-level quote: A letter proposal accompanied by a product brochure
Turnaround time: no more than twenty-four hours

B-level quote: A (brief) formal proposal that relies heavily on boilerplate
Turnaround time: no more than seventy-two hours

C-level quote: A formal proposal for a project of extraordinary scope or one that requires extensive research and development work or that involves complicated costing, or both
Turnaround time: several days to several months

What about charging for a proposal? Does that ever make sense? Usually it doesn't. The potential client will probably refuse to consider such a request. Besides, many quotes can be handled simply and quickly with just a letter or a letter accompanied by a small amount of supporting detail. This kind of quick turnaround quote requires minimal effort, and charging for it would be pointless.

However, there are times when you may be tempted to attach a bill to your proposal. For example, from a financial standpoint, you might be justified in charging for proposals that:

- Require thousands of dollars worth of effort with a low probability of receiving an order because of the client's apparent indecision or lack of commitment
- Involve R&D or design work that is highly specialized or even unique to the given project and that will not likely result in an order
- Are developed for a client who refuses to sign a nondisclosure agreement

What options do you have in such cases? I'd recommend going back to the bid/no bid analysis, asking yourself how strongly you want to compete for this work. If you're interested but not truly eager, you might be able to respond with a proposal that calls for doing the work in phases, with Phase I being a funded design study to figure out how to do the subsequent phases.

Or you could respond with a two-volume proposal. Volume One would contain the executive summary, general information about the proposed project or system, and information on management. That part would be free to the customer. Volume Two would contain the detailed design and specifications and would be available to the client on a fee basis, perhaps with the fee being deducted from the project costs if you win the contract.

## Assemble the Proposal Team

Once you have determined that you do indeed wish to proceed, you should establish an effective proposal team and clearly define the team members' responsibilities. At the minimum, an effective proposal team must have three key members. The roles can overlap somewhat, but it's a good idea to keep responsibilities as clearly defined as possible.

The three essential members are:

### *Proposal Manager*

Qualifications:

- Self-starter
- Leader
- Marketing knowledge and ability
- In-house communication and negotiation skills
- Strong cost "conscience"
- Solid, applications-oriented product knowledge

Experience:

- Field experience:
  —Customer relations
  —Sales
  —Installation or maintenance

- Project management experience
- Negotiation skills

Responsibilities:

- Helps develop the proposal strategy, and executes it in the form of the finished proposal:
  —Develops the appropriate response/solution to target
  —Assures the technical accuracy of the proposal
  —Takes responsibility for getting the proposal out on time
- Gathers and monitors cost data
- Controls the cost of proposal development ($/page)

### Technical Expert

Qualifications:

- Solid technical ability combined with creativity
- Outstanding product knowledge
- Good communication skills

Experience:

- Extensive systems-oriented experience
- PC- or CAD-literate

Responsibilities:

- Creates conceptual design of the proposal (or a designated part)
- Gathers and synthesizes design data
- Gathers cost data relevant to the pricing of the bid
- Writes the response to the RFP's specifications
- Develops the compliance matrix

### Writer/Graphics Expert

Qualifications:

- Outstanding writing skills
- PC-literate

Experience:

- Business or journalism background with an emphasis on crisp, clear communication

- Marketing or advertising experience
- Desktop publishing knowledge

Responsibilities:

- Helps determine proposal strategies
- Produces copy for front sections of proposals—cover letters and executive summaries, in particular
- Helps create and maintain textual data bases
- Edits drafts and finished documents
- Oversees production of final proposals

## Do Initial Review and Screening

Whenever possible, RFPs, RFQs (requests for quotes), and other inquiries should be reviewed and approved by a competition committee or other management. Normally, an account executive or field sales representative will already be familiar with the request and will be able to provide valuable information about the decisionmaker, the client's business position, the factors driving the RFP, and other important issues. In fact, it may be approporate to have the account executive function as the proposal manager. The project can also be assigned to someone else, depending on the person's experience and availability. Once the inquiry has been reviewed and a decision has been made to bid on it, resources should be made available to the proposal manager.

## Develop a Solution

If the appropriate level of response (that is, A, B, or C) has not been determined by management, the proposal manager should make that determination by analyzing the inquiry in more detail.

The proposal manager, in consultation with other management and the writer, should review the RFP or opportunity in detail, using the seven-step approach described in Chapter 5. The team should next analyze the decisionmaker as precisely as possible and then define the marketing strategy most likely to appeal successfully to that person. The proposal manager should assess the company's competitive strengths as they apply to the specific inquiry so that these strengths can be leveraged in the proposal. Likewise, the proposal manager should determine which uniqueness factors can be stressed in the proposal.

All of this analytical information forms the basis of the cover letter and the executive summary of the proposal. At this point, the writer can begin to produce these elements of the proposal.

## Develop a Storyboard Proposal

Simultaneous with starting the executive summary and cover letter, work should begin on developing the concept design and storyboarding the overall proposal. The concept design is the solution described in the proposal; description of the concept design normally occupies the majority of the technical section of the proposal. As the concept design is developed and defined by the technical expert, pricing—including estimates of required material and work/hours—should be derived from the technical description. Most of this development work is handled by the technical expert and the proposal manger, although they will need to call on the resources of other groups in large or complex proposals.

## Assemble and Review the Draft

The writer pulls together the various contributions and assembles all the pieces of the proposal. The proposal team, consisting of the proposal manager, the technical expert, the writer, and other contributors, reviews the draft for technical and pricing accuracy. It also reviews the persuasive marketing direction in light of any new insights from customer reviews or sales information. (Tips on reviewing the draft follow.)

On large projects, it can be extremely productive to set up

two teams, each of which produces a distinct proposal and then reviews the other team's efforts critically. This process can generate creativity, depth of analysis, and a much stronger final effort. Handled badly, it can also generate rabid competitiveness, bitterness, and egotism. The worst example of mismanaging the two-team approach that I know of occurred at a company that informed the teams at the outset that the team producing the better proposal would be rewarded with bonuses and promotions, while the team producing the loser would be fired! Not only did that stupid decision breed anxiety and stress, it also set up a situation in which it was impossible to take advantage of the strengths of both efforts.

## Revise the Draft

The writer/graphics expert incorporates all changes on the basis of the review.

## Perform a Management Review

At this point, management outside the proposal team may need to review the proposal. It's vital that these reviewers understand the basis for the strategic decisions and audience orientation that have led to the particular proposal format and style they're reviewing. Management must look outside its own prejudices when reviewing. Its value to the process lies primarily in reviewing the proposal for general content, pricing accuracy, and probable marketing performance.

Upper levels of management must refrain from second-guessing the proposal team at this point. The tendency in too many companies is for some vice-president to exercise ego and pull rank, demanding complete rewrites on proposals at the last moment. Clearly, that's asinine behavior. If the proposal team has been assembled carefully and given sound information, if it's properly trained, if it has done a thorough job of analzying the client organization, the decisionmakers, and the opportunity, then the proposal it will produce is far better than a proposal generated by some individual out of his or her head. And the team's effort is the one that's most likely to win the job.

Often, a top-level manager reacts negatively to a proposal and demands changes, not because the proposal is wrong, but because it has been done in a style that doesn't appeal to that particular manager's own personality style or assumptions.

### Protecting Your Proprietary Interests

Making sure the customer doesn't appropriate your ideas and shop them elsewhere is critical to protecting your interests. I once wrote a proposal that outlined a complete training program to help transform technical project leaders into business managers. We didn't get the contract, but our curriculum did become the basis for what the company instituted. There was small comfort in that. In another instance, I developed a proposal in partnership with a production company for a training/orientation video. The topic was technically complex, even intimidating, yet it needed to be explained to a lay audience in clear terms. What's more, the video had to be interesting, entertaining, and human. From among more than 400 bidders for this project, our proposal made the final cut. Only three vendors were invited to make a presentation of their concepts. We made the presentation, but we didn't get the job. That was disappointing. Even worse, we later learned that our concept was handed to a relative of one of the firm's owners to produce.

If people choose to be unethical, there's not a lot you can do, except to learn from your experience and try to avoid bidding on one of their jobs again. However, it's more likely that you're dealing with people who are simply ignorant of the value of what you've proposed. Here are some steps you can take to protect yourself and your solution in that situation:

1. *Seek a nondisclosure agreement before submitting your proposal.* If the client signs such an agreement, you can feel confident that what you submit won't be shopped around to your competitors. On the other hand, if the client refuses, you

have at least been alerted to the situation and may want to present your solution in general terms.

2. *Include a proprietary statement on your proposal's title page or on the page immediately following the title page.* The statement can be brief, and it doesn't have to sound threatening or defensive. Something like this may work:

> This proposal contains proprietary information. Please do not reveal any of its contents to anyone not directly responsible for evaluating it without first obtaining written permission.

Check with your own attorney for proper wording. Clearly, a proprietary statement doesn't guarantee that potential clients won't take advantage of your openness and thoroughness. But at least they can't claim they didn't know better.

3. *Mark those pages that contain sensitive information with a footer indicating that the information is proprietary.* My own attorneys have told me that you should not mark every page proprietary, because obviously not every page really is. The result of doing so would be to invalidate the proprietary claims you make for the crucial parts of the proposal. In general, your system design, solution description, creative idea, and pricing can be marked proprietary. Implementation schedules, management resumes, the executive summary, and similar general information cannot. Again, check with your own legal counsel.

4. *Submit your proposal at deadline.* Obviously, you can't submit it late, because then you're probably going to be rejected out of hand. But there's no reason to submit it early, either.

A couple of years ago I worked with a major software company in developing a response to one of the most complicated, detailed RFPs we'd ever seen. It was more than four hundred pages long and consisted mostly of the statement of work. Analyzing all of that, developing a strong, competitive response, and getting it written was an enormous challenge—particularly since vendors were being given only four weeks to respond. Through effective project management and the use of some techniques for automating the process, we were done on time. Meanwhile, several of the other bidders had petitioned the client to extend the deadline, a petition that was finally granted.

"Let's send ours in anyway," argued a couple of members of the proposal team. "It'll show that we're more competent than they are, that we can manage a project and get it done on time."

Makes sense in a way, doesn't it? In the end, though, we didn't do it. We submitted it to arrive when everybody else's did. The reason was that one of our key competitors was a subsidiary of the client organization. Since our bid was extremely innovative, we didn't want others to see it because they might learn too much from it. It was a matter of protecting our proprietary interests.

You should follow this rule with your proposal. If, by some miracle, you do finish the proposal early, wait until it's due before submitting it. If your proposal is sitting around on the client's desk and your competitors happen to drop in for a chat, it's possible that information in your proposal can leak into the wrong hands. Any well-trained account executive masters the art of reading upside down. Even a little hint, a slip of the tongue, a nuance, could be of value to your competitor.

5. *Limit distribution of the proposal.* Provide only as many copies as the RFP specifies or as the client requests. Shipping ten or fifteen copies of a proposal is courting disaster. Obviously, there's nothing to keep the client from making copies for its own use, but that's where steps 1 and 2 come in.

6. *Don't tell the client everything, and don't include things the client doesn't really need to know yet.* If you've ever seen a packet-switching network diagram, you've seen the cloud that "conceals" how the data is bundled and transferred. You can put your most sensitive information behind a "cloud" by writing at a level of generality rather than a level of specificity. Talk about functions without describing in detailed operational terms exactly how those functions are handled.

If the RFP insists that you provide detail, you have to do

it. Otherwise you can be thrown out of the bidding process as nonresponsive. What I'm urging you to do, however, is to resist the temptation to put in all the neat technical detail if you don't have to. That may be difficult for you, particularly if you're a technical person by training and disposition. In that case, you probably love the details and probably believe they're the most interesting and convincing part of the proposal. Trust me, they're not.

Another mistake I've seen is to provide a detailed price list in a proposal for a complex system. By including the price of every component, down to the smallest piece of coaxial cable or the tiniest bolt, you are essentially giving your client a shopping list. He or she can now bypass you, go to resellers or to your competitors, and buy the system you have envisioned. You don't make a dime.

The other danger you face when you provide extremely detailed pricing is that the client may start nit-picking. "Why do I need three sets of koozles? I'll only be using two. Why is this widget combined with a thermocoupler? That's not really necessary, is it?" Even if every pricing decision you've made is absolutely correct, the client may drive you crazy with objections and reservations. You're better off grouping your pricing elements into broad categories whenever possible.

7. *Consider asking a fee in return for technical specifications.* For huge proposals involving lots of design work or any other major investment of time and resources, some companies charge for the technical volume. The client gets the executive summary and the nonproprietary parts of the proposal without obligation but must pay a fee to obtain the details of the solution. Usually that fee is applied toward the costs of the project if the vendor is awarded the contract.

This can be a tough one to sell, especially if nobody in your industry is doing it. On the other hand, it certainly seems fair. It forces the client to get serious about the review process, and it clearly communicates that what it is receiving is the equivalent of a comprehensive design study, the kind that consulting organizations charge big bucks to perform.

8. *Build your recommended solution so that it includes a number of key "uniqueness factors"*—things that make you, your services,

and your company different from anybody else out there. If there are no uniqueness factors, the client might as well look at the pricing page, compare bottom lines, and order. But if you're selling a service, a solution that involves integrating components, if you're going to be installing, training, managing, or researching, there are uniqueness factors. Only the most basic commodity-level selling doesn't involve some kind of uniqueness factors. Or, more accurately, only the most unimaginative proposal writers fail to recognize the uniqueness factors inherent in their bid.

Your company is the biggest in the industry? Then you probably have a wealth of experience and resources that make you unique. Your company is brand new? Then you're small enough to be flexible and completely responsive to the client. Maybe your senior management will be involved in the project; maybe you have leading edge technology. Those factors make you unique.

I urge people who attend my proposal writing workshops to create a file of uniqueness factors, looking not only at products and the features of what they're selling, but also at aspects of their company: its culture, its resources, its quality program, its training, whatever. Keep the file updated regularly. As conditions change, as the company grows or reorganizes, as products or services are overhauled, revise your list of uniqueness factors.

Bear in mind that these factors work only if you can structure them as integral parts of the proposal. If they're just marketing hype, they won't protect your proposal from competitive raids. But if you can propose a solution that incorporates factors that are truly unique, nobody else can touch you. Even if they read your proposal, others can't do anything about it.

## Have the Proposal Printed

After any final changes or corrections are incorporated, the proposal goes into production. The final copy is printed and bound in sufficient quantities for delivery to the customer.

Printing should be done on a laser printer. The binding should be distinctive and professional. Beyond that, you should develop standards and guidelines that will create a distinctive "look and feel" for your proposals and then adhere to them.

Should you use color, elaborate graphics, and other impressive production techniques? It depends primarily on the audience, and to a lesser extent on the image you're trying to create. The use of expensive production techniques may suggest that you're an elite provider of services but may also suggest that you're expensive. Proposals being submitted to the government or to other public sector agencies shouldn't be too elaborate. Such techniques may be construed as wasteful.

## Deliver or Present the Proposal

Decide on the best way to present the proposal to the customer. Obviously, you'll have to make this decision in light of any input received from the customer. For example, many federal government RFPs specify delivery dates, times, and even acceptable modes of delivery. The vendor is not allowed to speak to any reviewers when delivering the proposal, and there is no opportunity after the final bidder's conference to speak to the decisionmakers.

In the private sector, it's more likely that you'll be allowed to deliver your written proposal in the context of an in-person presentation. Whenever you have that opportunity, take it! Face-to-face contact is the easiest way to build rapport, explore for problem areas, and move to closure.

## Perform a Win/Loss Analysis

This is the part of the process that gets neglected most often. After spending the time and money to produce a proposal, very few people bother to find out what worked and what didn't. But what information could be more important?

After the customer has made the buying decision, an

independent party should follow up to find out how effective the proposal was as a marketing tool, perhaps by asking the decisionmaker to complete an evaluation form such as that shown in Figure 8-2. It's important that this analysis be performed by people not directly involved with the project. After all, if the writer performs the analysis, it's not likely that the evidence will indicate that the proposal lost because of poor structure or confusing writing. A good candidate to perform the win/loss analysis is a market research group, if you can afford one.

Any information that you can obtain about what the decisionmaker liked or disliked about your proposal should be stored in a marketing data base. The next time you prepare a proposal for the same client, you'll have a valuable head start on the job.

## The Internal Review Process

When reviewing the proposal drafts, it's important to look at them from the point of view of the decisionmaker. It's also important to have somebody look at the proposal with a fresh pair of eyes. There are few tasks harder than editing your own work, primarily because you know exactly what you meant to say and, as a result, may not notice that you unintentionally said something entirely different.

When reviewing your proposal, try to look at it both objectively and subjectively. An objective review should focus on four key areas: content, organization, effective use of language, and correctness.

### 20 Questions for Reviewing Proposals

#### Content

1. Is the basic idea or recommendation a good one?
2. Are the facts accurate?
3. Is the recommendation or idea supported by sufficient evidence or examples?

(text continued on page 90)

**Figure 8-2.** Sample evaluation form.

---

### HOW DID WE DO?

Our firm is continually looking for ways to serve you better. Your answers to this questionnaire will help us in that mission. Won't you please give us a few minutes of your time?

Proposal Number/Title: _____

Your Company Name: _____

Your Name (Optional): _____

Phone Number (Optional): _____

### A. PROPOSAL FORMAT

   1. Did our proposal correctly respond to your request?    **Yes No**
      If not, where did we fail?

      _____

      _____

      _____

   2. Was our proposal well organized?    **Yes No**
      If not, how could we improve its organization?

      _____

      _____

      _____

   3. Was our proposal easy to understand?    **Yes No**
      If not, how could we clarify it?

      _____

      _____

      _____

   4. Did we provide enough detail on our products and services?  **Yes No**

   5. After receiving the proposal, did you have to ask us for
      more information?    **Yes No**

   6. Was the proposal:
      A) Too long/detailed   B) Too short/cursory   C) Just right

   7. Do you feel we responded to your request in a
      timely manner?    **Yes No**

## B. PRICING

1. Did we provide sufficient pricing detail?                 **Yes  No**

2. Was our pricing too detailed?                             **Yes  No**

3. Did we forget to include any pricing?                     **Yes  No**
   If Yes, what did we leave out?

   _____

   _____

   _____

4. Did we adequately explain our pricing?                    **Yes  No**

5. How did our pricing compare to other companies
   responding to the same request?

   A) Higher      B) Lower      C) About the same

## C. PROPOSAL EFFECTIVENESS

1. Did our proposal result in the placement of an order
   with our firm?                                            **Yes  No**

2. What were your key reasons for selecting/not selecting us?

   _____

   _____

   _____

   _____

   _____

   _____

   _____

**NOTE:** AFTER COMPLETING THE QUESTIONNAIRE, PLEASE
RETURN IT TO US IN THE ENCLOSED SELF-
ADDRESSED/STAMPED ENVELOPE.

## . . . And thank you!

4. Is the solution being proposed clearly worthwhile?
5. Is there too much vagueness, abstraction, or generalization?
6. Is there too much clutter of details without an overview or sense of perspective?
7. Is the proposal client-centered rather than product-centered?

## Organization

8. Is the proposal unified? Is there one central strategy to which everything is related?
9. Are the parts arranged in a coherent, logical sequence?
10. Do the cover letter and executive summary attract the reader's interest?
11. Is there closure to each major section?
12. Does each section of the proposal seem complete?
13. Is each section organized by means of the persuasive paradigm?

## Effective Language

14. Are the sentences clear and readable?
15. Are the words used correctly?
16. Is the proposal concise?
17. Is the writing appropriate to the audience's personality and expertise?

## Correctness

18. Are there mistakes in grammar, usage, spelling, or typing?
19. Are there mistakes in names, dates, addresses, or other details?
20. Is it neat, professional-looking, and easy to read?

Objective criteria can take you only part of the way. You also need to consider the subjective reactions your proposal will produce in the reader. To gauge that, ask someone who hasn't been part of the proposal team, who doesn't have too much technical knowledge, and who has the guts to be completely honest with you—ideally, someone who's as much like the decisionmaker as possible—to read the proposal. Then, put your ego on hold, and ask the following questions:

*After reading only the cover letter and executive summary:*

1. What did you think about or feel as you read this material?
2. Did any words or phrases catch your attention or stand out in any way (good or bad)?
3. What is the key message you get from this section? What do you now expect the whole proposal to say?
4. What ideas, beliefs, or feelings do you bring to this material that could influence the way you read it?
5. On the basis of these opening elements, what impressions do you have of the writer?
6. At this early stage, are you for or against the writer?
7. What do you wish you knew at this point that's not available in the material you just read?

*After reading the whole proposal:*

8. Are there any sentences, paragraphs, or sections you especially like?
9. Are there any dull or confusing areas?
10. What impression do you have now of the writer? of the proposal?

As people give you their reactions to the proposal, listen uncritically. Most of us tend to start preparing excuses and explanations as to why it "has to be this way" even before our critics finish telling us what they think. Rather than wasting time talking, invest time in listening. After all, you won't have a chance to explain to the actual evaluators and decisionmakers who read your proposal why it "has to be this way."

## How Evaluators Do It

How do the people who regularly read proposals approach the task? Are they more objective than subjective? Do they approach every proposal as a brand-new experience? What do they look for?

From interviews with consultants and evaluators who have had a lot of experience in this area, here's what I've learned. Evaluators do compare responses from various vendors, even though they're not supposed to. What that means is that you'd better give some thought to analyzing why your solution is a better choice than others the evaluators may see. Think in terms of responsiveness to the entire need or problem and think in terms of return on investment. However, don't disparage the competition.

Evaluators are influenced by past experience with each vendor. If you know who the evaluator is and if you know that he or she has certain negative attitudes toward you or your company because of past experience, it would be wise to address that experience indirectly. How can you do that? Suppose that, on a previous contract, your firm had problems meeting quality control requirements. In the new proposal, a section that discusses steps your firm has taken to improve quality might help alleviate the evaluator's concerns (assuming that you're being honest, of course).

Evaluators get tired of evaluating. After the first few proposals, the job can become both boring and fatiguing. As a result, I urge you to keep your proposal as short as possible. I realize that lots of people believe they have to give the client "bulk," but think about your own reaction: If you had two proposals on your desk, one of which was 150 pages long while the other was 45 pages, which would you pick up first? Most of us would look at the short one first.

Also, it pays to make your proposal as easy to read as possible. Use a clear, substantive table of contents, lots of headings and subheadings, and bullet points. Print it on a laser printer, and use a clean, crisp typeface. Evaluators appreciate proposals that are well organized, with a compliance matrix and other format devices that make it easy to find and refer to the information. These features encourage skimming and give you the chance to reinforce your key message. A proposal that's easier to read than another will appear to make more sense. Subliminal factors, such as the clarity of the writing, the ease of using and reading the proposal, and the inclusion of visuals, can also influence an evaluation, even when the evaluators are using a numerical scoring system.

Evaluators report that their key evaluation criterion is usually responsiveness to the key issues and requirements of the RFP. Next in importance are apparent technical and/or managerial competence and cost, in that order.

Proposals that simply promise to comply with a requirement are treated harshly by most evaluators, who need the sense of security that comes from specificity in this area. They look more favorably upon proposals that tell how the vendor will meet the requirement.

Evaluators also tend to be harsh with vendors who take things for granted or whose attitude seems arrogant or patronizing. If you're working for a globally recognized company, one that's universally acknowledged as a leader in its field, if you're a member of a research laboratory at an internationally famous university, you may feel that it's unnecessary to answer all the picky little questions that the little guys have to answer. You're right. It is unnecessary. Unless you want to win the competition, of course.

Once an evaluator considers a proposal to be nonresponsive, the evaluations get tougher and tougher. I suppose it's a little like judging figure skating or gymnastics. After a couple of slips, the performer doesn't get the benefit of the doubt anymore.

# 9

# Developing a Winning Strategy

What is strategy, and how does it apply to writing a proposal?

In the military, strategy is the grand plan by which a commander attempts to exploit the enemy's weaknesses by capitalizing on his own strengths. In other words, strategy is how you maximize your chance to win. It's the same basic thing in proposal writing. Strategy for you as a proposal writer is the intelligent application of your understanding of three things:

1. The client's business needs
2. Your business's strengths
3. Your competitor's strengths and weaknesses

Understanding these factors enables you to produce the leverage necessary to achieve your business objectives.

## What Strategy Isn't

Choosing an effective winning strategy should be a process of analysis and reason. That's why they call it "strategic thinking." (I'll allow you the option of playing a hunch now and then. Everybody has a certain amount of intuition, and it's worth respecting.) The one thing you can't allow is to base your strategy on an emotional reaction out of fear or anxiety.

Proposal writers who don't think through the issue of

strategy usually come up with no strategy at all. And people who react out of fear or anxiety usually fail to develop an effective one. As a result, they commit one or more of the "seven deadly sins" of proposal writing:

1. Trying to be everything to everybody; taking a "shotgun" approach
2. Making loud claims but failing to back them up with substance
3. Offering a proposal that responds more to a competitor's position than it does to the client's need
4. Presenting a "canned" solution
5. Writing a technical description instead of a persuasive proposal
6. Producing a "cost paranoia proposal," one that focuses exclusively on payback and the cost/benefit ratio
7. Failing to address the client's needs in the proposal

These mistakes undercut the persuasive power of your proposal. To avoid them:

1. Be specific. Have a clearly focused strategy.
2. Provide sufficient, relevant supporting materials, and focus them on how your solution will meet the client's needs. Don't waste paper with glowing descriptions of your company's reputation, corporate philosophy, history, or product features.
3. Stress your company's uniqueness factors.
4. Write with a client focus so that the proposal as a whole sounds tailored to the client's needs, and tie the proposed solution to the client's business needs so that the solution also sounds tailored.
5. Don't lose sight of the controlling purpose of the proposal—*persuasion*.
6. Put discussions of cost and return on investment in their proper perspective for each client.
7. Finally, focus tightly on your client's needs, and don't allow your vision to waver!

## The Client's Business Needs

Of the three elements that determine strategy, the client's need is the most important. By now, this shouldn't come as a big surprise to you. In fact, by now you probably feel like you've been pounded over the head with this "client-oriented" stuff. Fine. It's pretty much the key point in the *Persuasive Business Proposals* solution.

You'll face the biggest difficulties when the client issues nothing but a detailed specification sheet and simply calls for bids against the specs. In such circumstances, the client may be trying to turn the process into a commodity purchase, focusing exclusively on price. That's not a real smart move on the client's part, and it may create problems for you, particularly if you're not the vendor with the lowest price. Similarly, the client's use of a consultant can complicate the process of developing an effective strategy. However, the fact remains that defining the client's business need is the essential first step toward developing your winning strategy. You can respond to an RFP with 100 percent technical compliance and with the lowest cost and still not win the contract because you failed to address the customer's real concerns. These concerns may be separate from the product or service requirements specified in the RFP, but they are always the driving force that guides the selection of a winner.

Using the seven-step approach described in Chapter 5, identify to the best of your ability the business issues behind the customer's technical requirements. Your knowledge of the client organization, its history, and its objectives will be your best guide in identifying business issues. In addition, you can look for insight to the RFP itself; especially significant are the presence of unanswered questions or unresolved problems, requests for alternatives, and the presence of vague guidelines.

## Your Business's Strengths

When you walk down the aisle of your local grocery store where the cold cereal is stocked, what do you see? A wide assortment, obviously. Dozens of different kinds of cereal, each with something that makes it different from every other kind. These differences establish an identity in the marketplace for the product. As a potential customer, you evaluate them in terms of what you want or need and what they have to offer. This one is presweetened. That one has extra fiber. Over here we have one with a mixture of grains plus fruit. And so on.

You're not selling cereal, obviously, but you face the same basic challenge that Kellogg's and General Foods face. You have to appeal to your client's "taste," have to establish some difference between yourself and the others, and you have to do it in a way that stands out. In my proposal writing workshops, I lead people through a brief exercise to get them started in this process. But it's something that you can do yourself, and it's something that has to be maintained to be of value.

First, take a piece of paper and put your company's name at the top. Head separate sheets of paper with the names of your key products or services. Next, under each heading list all of the things that make your company or your offerings stand out in the marketplace. You're trying to uncover all of the major differences or discriminators that separate your company from the competition. In particular, try to identify the "uniqueness factors"—the things about your company, product, or service that are truly one of a kind.

Some uniqueness factors are generic: having the most reliable product line in the industry as measured by independent testing; offering superior performance; providing the most generous maintenance/service agreement; featuring the lowest pricing, unparalleled expandability, open systems design, or unlimited upgradability; having the longest history, the most experience, or the widest range of development tools. These uniqueness factors might be included in any proposal because they're so broad. Other uniqueness factors might be specific to a given RFP: for example, the mix of features available on a particular piece of equipment, or the experience of a given project manager in handling exactly the kind of project upon which you're bidding. The point is that to the extent you have identified factors that truly are unique, you have identified factors that give you a competitive edge.

Allow yourself plenty of time to develop your lists, and don't worry about their being absolutely correct. The lists are a starting point. As your company, your products and services, and the marketplace evolve, the lists will change. Some of the offerings that were uniquely yours will become available from your competitors. On the other hand, you will be able to add new features, products, services, and factors to your lists as you and your company grow.

## Your Competitor's Strengths and Weaknesses

Your final challenge is to look closely at what your competitors are offering and prepare "uniqueness factor" lists for them. You won't need to do as thorough a job as you did on your own list, obviously; nor would you ever be able to, barring some act of industrial espionage. But the more you can learn about what's out there competing against you, the better you'll understand how to position your own company.

The usual sources of information about your competitors are their own literature, trade show displays, and comments from your clients and theirs. You can also gather a boatload of information from reading your competitors' proposals. Take the opportunity to look at how they did it whenever you can do so without behaving unethically. For example, request copies of the nonproprietary parts of winning proposals submitted by others on government jobs after the contract has been awarded. Or simply request a debriefing from the decision-maker. Reading your competitors' proposals can open your eyes, particularly if you can do it in a nonjudgmental way. Rather than getting angry, resentful, or indignant about claims you think are inaccurate, ask yourself. "What can I learn from the way this was positioned?"

## Four Strategic Options

Having performed this analysis, you now can formulate a strategy that capitalizes on your strengths, minimizes your weaknesses, and does the opposite for your competitors. You can make the process as simple or as complicated as you wish. Personally, I like simple. As a result, I usually think in terms of just four basic strategic options. There are others, but I have yet to see a case where it really paid to get too clever or too precise in formulating the general strategy. The reason is that the strategy of your proposal is analogous to the basic theme in a piece of music. The theme needs to be simple enough— just a few notes or a musical phrase—so that the composer can return to it and work variations on it repeatedly without the music becoming boring. Finally, you'll find it much easier to assign sections of a major proposal to the members of a team, confident that they can all write their parts with a consistent strategic focus, if the statement of the strategy is as simple and clear as possible.

The four strategic options that I recommend you consider are:

- Cost
- Quality
- Technology
- Competitive

If you decide to use the *cost* strategy, you want to write your proposal—and that means every section, every page, every paragraph—so that it convinces the decisionmaker that:

- Your solution is the least expensive.
- Your solution is the best value.
- Your solution offers the highest return on his or her investment.
- Your solution saves the most money.
- Your solution saves something even more valuable than money—such as time.

Use the *quality* strategy when you have decided that your proposal has the best chance of winning if the decisionmaker recognizes that:

- Your solution offers the highest quality.
- Your solution is the most reliable.
- Your solution provides the most measurable controls over processes.
- Your solution will yield the highest customer satisfaction.

If you adopt the *technology* strategy, you have decided that your proposal has the best chance of winning if the decisionmaker recognizes that:

- Your solution is the most advanced.
- Your solution offers the most flexibility.
- Your solution eliminates or automates the most labor-intensive operations.
- Your solution capitalizes on leading-edge developments.

If you choose the *competitive* strategy, you have decided that your proposal has the best chance of winning if the decision-maker recognizes that:

- Your solution offers the best mix of desirable elements.
- Your solution gives the client an advantage in the marketplace.
- Your solution is superior because it comes from you.

Another advantage of limiting the number of strategies you work with is that you can now go back to your lists of uniqueness factors and categorize them. Examine each factor, asking, "What basic strategy or strategies does this support?" For example, if you design flexible machining cells using control language that permits the user to link the cell with any kind of controller on the market, that's a technology advantage, isn't it? But it could also be a cost advantage, because it may mean that the client can use existing equipment instead of replacing it with something new. Or, if your consulting firm involves senior partners in the direct supervision of every project, regardless of size, that's a potential quality advantage. It might also be a competitive advantage.

As you analyze your lists of uniqueness factors, you can

put a symbol in the margin next to each item, according to its category. For points that support a cost strategy, for example, you can put a $; a Q can go next to any entry supporting a quality strategy. Then, once you've chosen your overall strategy, you can pull out your lists of uniqueness factors for the company as a whole and for the given products and services you're combining in this bid and look for those that will support your position. The better you do this job, the more truly unique the factors you choose to illustrate and support your case, the more impregnable your proposal. And if you can fold in the uniqueness factors as integral parts of your solution, not merely as bells and whistles, you'll have given yourself a competitive advantage; your proposal will now stand out as clearly different from your competitors'.

What if you choose the wrong strategy? What if a different strategy actually would have been more persuasive? Don't worry about it. The mere fact that you have a unified approach will make your proposal sound more convincing than the bulk of proposals the decisionmaker receives. The point isn't so much choosing the right strategy. Rather, the key point is this: *One clearly defined strategy must dominate the proposal.*

## Giving Your Strategy a Twist

You can build your proposal's strategy on either a positive or a negative foundation. Positive strategies are based on the value of *gain*. Your objective here is to persuade the client that what you are proposing offers him or her the greatest amount of gain of all the courses of action available. Negative strategies are based on *fear*. Your purpose is to alert the client to the problems (or even disasters) that are possible unless certain measures are taken. You strengthen your competitive position by pointing out that only you or your company is uniquely qualified to take those measures.

Which approach is better? It depends on your position, what you have to offer, and what you think is most likely to motivate the decisionmaker. There's nothing inherently sleazy or unethical about basing your strategy on fear, as long as you're being honest in what you say. For example, if you're offering a trenching system that is particularly well suited to sandy soil and if your competitor's systems are not as safe or secure in sandy soil, you're not being an alarmist to point out that, since the client's construction site is in a sandy area, your system will work better.

## Strategy as Determined by the Decisionmaker

If your analysis of strengths and weaknesses leaves you undecided about which strategy to adopt in your proposal, take a look at the decisionmaker. In particular, look at the issues of that person's role in the decision process and personality type.

What role does the key evaluator play? Given that role, which strategy is your best choice? For example, if your proposal is going directly to the ultimate authority, your best choice—in the absence of evidence to the contrary—is a cost-based strategy. On the other hand, if the decisionmaker is the user of your product or service, a quality-based strategy, particularly one that emphasizes reliability, ruggedness, ease of maintenance, and similar features, is most effective. For the gatekeeper, a technical strategy works best, especially if the proposal is oriented toward the particular technical criteria the gatekeeper will be using to evaluate it.

The personality type of the decisionmaker should also influence your choice of strategy. It's easy to get into stereotyped thinking in this area, so be careful. But consider these factors as general guidelines in formulating your strategy. In the absence of any other evidence, for example, you'd be reasonably justified in assuming that a pragmatic decisionmaker, the personality type that tends to be driven by bottom-line issues, is most likely to be persuaded by a cost or competitive strategy. A detail-oriented person may respond to a technology strategy, although this assumption is a little shakier. An accountant or comptroller is likely to be detail-oriented, for example, but at the same time very likely to be persuaded by cost factors. The consensus-oriented person takes buzzwords such as *service, support, continuity of the business relation-*

*ship, partnership,* and *win/win negotiating* seriously. As a result, a quality-based strategy may be your best choice for this kind of client. As for the visionary, it's hard to say. My own experience with the truly creative, entrepreneurial types suggests that your strategy should be based on whatever factors are most important to them.

## Business Realities and Your Strategy

Another factor to consider when you're choosing a dominant strategy is the overall business environment within which the client organization is operating. This business position is a key factor in determining your strategy.

▪ *Growth.* A growing client's decisions are driven primarily by the demands of keeping up with expanding sales or volume. To win business from a growing client, focus on the challenges posed by increasing sales or volume. For example, your proposal should indicate that the solution you offer will enable the client to increase productivity to keep pace with sales, decrease operating costs so that each sale is more profitable, or simplify the sales and delivery cycle to reduce waste.

If the company is in a growth pattern, the quality or technology strategies are usually your best choice, coupled with a positive orientation. If you do choose a technology strategy, be sure to focus on technology as it affects business issues such as productivity and throughput, not for its own sake.

▪ *Decline.* A declining client's decisions are generally driven by cost factors. A winning strategy must focus on improving the cost structure of operations, on eliminating waste, on automating labor-intensive processes, and on maximizing existing resources, all with the idea that money can then be put into efforts to stop the loss of market share. If the company is in decline, the cost strategy is usually your best choice. Consider using a negative spin.

▪ *Stable.* A stable client is usually the most difficult to sell to, because it has little motivation to change. There's not much pressure to upset the status quo. Increasing sales is desirable, but not if the costs increase in the process. Likewise, reducing costs is desirable, but not at the expense of sales or market share.

If the company is stable, your chances of making a sale are much lower no matter which strategy you use. Consider using a competitive strategy, particularly if you can create a sense of partnership or if you are able to develop a strong internal champion to help make your case.

## Overview of Proposal Strategies: Look for Competitive Advantage

By solving a significant problem or enabling a customer to capitalize on a major opportunity, you provide him or her with competitive advantage in the marketplace. Competitive advantage is the most desired, most precious commodity in business. By providing it, you become your client's partner, not merely a vendor.

In choosing your strategy, look for the approach that leads toward competitive advantage for the client. Here are a few factors to keep in mind:

- True, long-term competitive advantage derives from solutions, not products. No matter how innovative products or services may be initially, they will eventually become commodities. The only component of a solution that cannot be incorporated in your competitor's recommendations is you. Your ability to develop creative applications that dramatically improve business operations is the indispensable key.
- Your proposed solution must provide clearly superior added value in one important area over competitive solutions and over doing nothing. Ideally, this added value should be most obvious or significant in the client's highest priority goal area.
- Your proposed solution must at least equal competitive solutions in all other respects. Basing your proposal on

a cost strategy does not mean you can ignore quality issues.

Guard against the tendency to provide an overengineered or overpackaged solution. Such a proposal undercuts the competitiveness of what you have to offer.

# 10

# Writing From the Right Brain: Getting Your Ideas Organized

For some people, getting ideas organized into some kind of flowing outline is no problem. They seem to produce concepts quickly, easily, and logically. But, as the song says, that's some people. That may not be you or me. In fact, one of the questions I've been asked most frequently in proposal writing seminars is, "How can I write my proposals faster?"

The answer to that question depends on what happens when you try to write. There may be structural or management problems in your company that impede the flow of information so that you lack the necessary facts. Or you may encounter difficulties in delegating work and then getting it back on time. Usually, though, what we are talking about is more basic. Most often, people take a long time to write because they have a hard time figuring out what they want to say and how they want to say it. Often they know *what* they want to say; they just don't know *how* to say it.

The chief engineer at one of the world's largest engineering companies told me that he hated to write proposals. "When I look at an engineering problem," he said, "I can immediately see the answer. But the answer is a totality. It's one complete thing. The problem is, I can't communicate it that way. I have to take this solid, complete answer and stuff it through a funnel so that it comes out one bit at a time. And to make it worse, the bits have to drip out in just the right order or none of it counts!" In expressing his frustration, he had concocted a perfect visual image for the process he was going through.

About fifteen years ago, research into a particularly serious form of epilepsy revealed a startling fact: The two halves (or hemispheres) of the brain function quite differently from each other. The left hemisphere in most people controls most forms of sequential thinking, including language. The right hemisphere controls visualization and holistic or global thinking. (This hemispheric differentiation is sometimes reversed in left-handed people.) Equally as interesting is the fact that people tend to be dominant to one hemisphere or the other. Just as they prefer to pick up a pen and write a check with one hand over the other, they prefer to process information and "think" using the cognitive patterns of one hemisphere over the other.

What does this have to do with writing proposals? Just this: If you are a right-brain thinker, you may be able to conceptualize quickly and creatively but then have an excruciatingly difficult time communicating your thoughts because communicating in language requires sequential processing. You have to put one word in front of another, one sentence ahead of the next, and it all has to flow logically and make sense. For the right-brain thinker, that's a two-step process, whereas for the left-brain thinker, it's an integral part of the thinking process itself.

No one would say that chief engineer I mentioned earlier was anything less than brilliant. But he was strongly oriented toward right-brain thinking. And if you have trouble getting your ideas organized and on the page, maybe you are, too.

## Proposal Storyboards

After hearing people describe their difficulties in organizing their thoughts in writing, I finally figured out a way to help right-brain proposal writers to get their ideas onto the page quickly. I call it "storyboarding" the proposal, because it attempts to use spatial or visual means of capturing ideas, the way a film or video producer uses sketches to trace the flow of a project.

Here are the steps to follow to get your ideas out of your head and onto the page:

*Step One.* Write on a blank sheet of paper the key *result* the client seeks as you understand it. Try to write that result in just a phrase or a brief sentence. To broaden your understanding, consider:

- What specific outcomes should this project produce?
- What specific objectives should this project realize? (Think in terms of technical, marketing, financial, and other objectives.)
- Which objectives are most important? What business needs do they address?

For example, if you're trying to write a proposal recommending that your client install an upgrade to an existing application or system, you might write down "ABC Technologies will be able to handle a larger volume of data on the same mainframe by installing our DataMaster System."

*Step Two.* Now, just brainstorm. Don't worry about logic or continuity at this point. Let the ideas flow at random. Ask yourself basic questions like "Who?" "Why?" "When?" Jot down the answers. Put down anything that occurs to you. Begin creating a web of related ideas, feelings, facts, and observations. And don't try to put down the first things first. Trying to get ideas down sequentially is the part of the old process that was killing you.

Some other questions you might ask so you can develop a complete picture:

- How can we define the result areas?
- What are the appropriate measurement indicators?
- What performance standards does the client want?
- What is the time frame for delivering these results?
- What is the cost?
- What is my solution?

This is an extremely useful technique when a proposal project is being handled by a team. Each person can contribute ideas as they occur. Don't exclude or reject anything that comes up.

*Step Three.* Draw lines connecting related ideas or facts. Connect the key points to the central idea that you wrote down first. These are the main spokes of your cognitive web. Expand on the ideas, getting more specific where you can.

*Step Four.* After taking a break from the process, look at your web of ideas and ask yourself what the audience needs to hear first. You've done your audience analysis work earlier, so you should be able to put yourself in the audience's place. What do you think will be most important to it? Put a "1" next to that key point. Then go on to enumerate the rest of your key points, the ones connected to the central idea. If there are supporting points under the key points, enumerate them the same way. Always ask what should come first from the audience's point of view.

At this point, you're probably going to have quite a mess. That's good. Now you can copy this mess neatly on a sheet of paper, putting point number one first, followed by its subpoints, and so on, in nice linear fashion right down the page. Presto! You have an outline for your document. And it was fairly painless, wasn't it?

The material you've generated is your outline for the executive summary or for a complete letter proposal. You can repeat the process for each section of the proposal as necessary, focusing on the technical specifications, functional specification, project plan, and cost analysis.

Does this method work? Yes! It really does. People have told me that it has cut their writing time on letter proposals from several hours to twenty or thirty minutes. Even some left-brain writers use it, because it also helps them become more creative. Try it.

# 11

# Formatting the Letter Proposal

The first thing you need to know is that there is no single, magical format that's correct for every proposal you write. Each proposal should be designed to communicate persuasively to a specific audience concerning a specific business situation. In fact, if you use the same format for every proposal, you'll probably be using the wrong format at least 75 percent of the time.

The letter proposal may be as brief as a single page. Usually it runs no more than three or four pages. The exact salutation you use, the particular letter style you choose (block, modified block, whatever), the complimentary close, none of that's really very important. What's important is that your letter proposal clearly address the essential elements of the persuasive paradigm described in Chapter 6:

1. *The client's need or problem.* Get right to the point. Don't waste time telling the client what kind of business he or she is in or what his or her business objectives are. Focus on a specific need or problem that is hurting the client's profitability or productivity.

It's possible to base your proposal on an opportunity. This is often the case in direct-mail campaigns. But remember that decisionmakers are much more motivated to act by needs and problems than they are by opportunities.

2. *The benefits of solving the problem or meeting the need.* You arouse the client's interest in the opening by pointing out a

real problem or need. You hold his or her interest by pointing out how much can be gained by addressing the problem or need.

Don't confuse the benefits of solving the business problem with the benefits of your product or service. (Those are more accurately called features and should be presented in the next section, where you detail your solution.) Quantify benefits whenever possible. The most appealing benefits are usually those that directly improve profitability.

3. *The solution.* The presentation of your solution should contain:

- A description of the product or service you are recommending
  —Tie it clearly to the client's needs.
  —Remember to stress your company's uniqueness factors.
- A brief consideration of alternative solutions
  —This shows thoroughness on your part, a true consultative attitude.
  —This also allows you to anticipate the competition's approach and point out its weakness without engaging in disparagement.
- A specific, clear recommendation to act
  —Too many proposals merely describe a solution; make sure you recommend it!

4. *The wrap-up.* In the wrap-up section of your letter proposal, you should address three key issues:

1. The cost/benefit ratio
   —Show the client that the benefits far outweigh the costs.
   —Include a consideration of intangible costs (training, reassignment of personnel) and of intangible benefits (better image, higher employee morale).
2. Special technical considerations
   —If there are exceptions, reservations, or special concerns, point them out here.
3. The implementation schedule
   —This can be handled as an attachment to your letter.

—In addition to presenting a time line and appropriate milestones, indicate responsibilities at each phase of implementation.

## A Few Tips on Writing Winning Letter Proposals

Here are a few suggestions for producing effective letter proposals:

1. *Don't let the tone become too stuffy.* Your tone will sound friendly and positive if you express your ideas from the reader's point of view.

2. *Avoid the clichés of business writing*—the hackneyed openings and closing that your reader has probably seen a hundred times before. In particular, avoid clichéd openings, such as, "I would like to take this opportunity to thank you for considering the enclosed . . . blah, blah, blah." Get to the point.

Also, avoid clichéd closings like, "If you have any questions, please feel free to call." That's a closing that's been done to death. So bury it. Don't use it. I know it's easy, and I know everyone does it, but think about what it says: Basically, it presupposes failure on your part. And it leaves any subsequent action entirely up to the reader. It even predicates that action on confusion. What a lousy way to end your proposal!

3. *Use a strong close.* Ask for the business. Remember, the final paragraph is your last chance to motivate the reader to do what you want him or her to do. Don't waste it with meaningless banalities such as, "Thanking you in advance for your cooperation" or "Let me know if I can be of any help."

To motivate the reader in the closing lines of the letter, return to your key selling strategy: cost, quality, technology, or competitive advantage. Tell the reader exactly what you want him or her to do. Remind the reader of the benefits of taking action. And try to make the action something that's easy to do—the easier the better.

Strong closings suggest specific action ("Just return the enclosed card and we'll arrange a free analysis of your inventory control procedures"), ask a question ("After all, if you can save $6,000 a month in computing costs, can you afford to say no?"), create time pressure ("The special pricing I have offered in this proposal will be available to you only for the next two weeks, so please don't hesitate"), or simply ask for the sale ("Please sign the enclosed contract and return it to us, so we can begin work on the project and you can begin seeing increased productivity on the shop floor").

Finally, close with confidence. Avoid expressions like "I hope that" and "If it would be all right." When you have said what you wanted to say—stop.

4. *Structure your proposal so that at least parts of it are intelligible to audiences at varying levels of technical sophistication.* This can be one of the most difficult tasks you face. How do you provide enough detail to meet the needs of the specialists without totally intimidating the less-informed readers?

A good technique is to design each part of the proposal in terms of two distinct components.

- The opening component is aimed at an "executive" audience. It provides an overview from the organizational point of view, and it consists of the first three elements of the letter proposal format—the statement of the problem, the payoff, and the solution. In other words, it gives the readers the "action information." Keep the writing itself fairly simple and direct.
- The discussion component is aimed at the specialists and looks at the problem from a technical point of view. It contains an introduction, the technical details, and the technical conclusions/recommendations. This material can be handled as the second half of the letter or as an attachment to the letter.

Each component should stand on its own. There may be selective redundancy between them, but not too much. And each component should move from general to particular in its discussion.

By structuring the proposal this way, you have created a document that can be used easily and successfully by every level of audience. The nonexperts can read the opening component in detail and skim the technical part. The technical types can do the opposite. And one or two people, perhaps those with management responsibilities for technical operations, can read, understand, and use both components. In essence, you're doing the same thing with this approach that you do in a formal proposal when you write an executive summary followed by the "body" of specific detail.

## SAMPLE LETTER PROPOSAL

[date]

Mr. Walter Giles
Mr. James Giles
Butter Creek Shipping, Inc.
Address
City

Gentlemen:

Strang, Wynch, and Winkle is pleased to submit this proposal to handle your accounting and related professional services. As a growing business in a highly competitive market, Butter Creek Shipping needs a solid partnership with its accounting firm, one that features personal service at a cost-effective price. That's exactly what we offer.

**Personal Service**

Strang, Wynch, and Winkle can bring some distinct advantages to the process of handling your audit. Perhaps most important, we will provide your business with the close attention it deserves. Unlike the typical national firms, Strang, Wynch, and Winkle will assign senior partners to handle the Butter Creek Shipping account.

In addition, as a medium-size firm, we have the flexibility and responsiveness to meet all deadlines, especially those imposed by third parties and regulators. We offer you the level of service and commitment that the national firms save for their largest clients. At the same time, we have the resources, specialized knowledge, and experience to handle complex assignments quickly.

We pride ourselves on providing quality service to every client. Like your own business, ours has achieved a solid record of growth by doing what it takes: working closely with our clients to develop business solutions, not merely to provide raw business data. Providing all services on a timely basis with continuity of personnel. Offering an impressive range of expertise in specialty areas often thought of as the domain of much larger firms. Taking a personal approach to each client and each task. Providing direct, immediate service carefully tailored to the client's needs. Personally involving our senior partners in providing service to our clients.

**Services We Will Provide**

The focus of our service will be on compiling the year-end reports necessary for compliance and on working with you to minimize tax liabilities both for the company and for you as owners.

We are proud of the quality of work we perform and of our commitment to each client's business success. We believe that well-conducted tax and audit services, performed by high-caliber professionals who use quality-oriented methods, integrated with an intelligent business plan, can become vital tools in helping you manage your business for success.

The specific services we will provide include:

- _____
- _____
- _____

*[Schedule of various tax services to be provided]*

## Lower Rates

Strang, Wynch, and Winkle will not only provide you with senior partner support, outstanding expertise, and quick responsiveness, we can do it at lower rates than the national firms.

As the attached fee schedule indicates, we will quote a fixed price for handling all tax returns and quarterly consultations billed on a per/hour basis.

In summary, we're eager to work with you on this project. And we're looking forward to forging a strong business partnership between our firms.


Sincerely,


[*name*]

# 12

# Formatting the Formal Proposal

Sometimes it's more appropriate to write a formal proposal than to submit a letter proposal. You may decide to do so, for example, if the document is too long (that is, more than four or five pages) to fit comfortably in the letter format, if it's proposing a costly or complicated solution, or if a formal, sectioned response has been mandated by the RFP to which you are responding.

Typically, a formal proposal contains the elements listed here. However, it doesn't have to contain all of them. In fact, it's a good idea to remind yourself that "less is more" when it comes to formal proposals. Keep it brief, keep it focused, and make it persuasive.

The components of a formal proposal include:

1. Cover letter
2. Title page
3. Proprietary statement (optional)
4. Table of contents
5. Executive summary
6. Body, perhaps including some of the following, presented in the order of their importance to the decision-maker:
   —Technical volume: details of the solution and recommended approach
   —Cost volume: explanation of the cost justification and return on investment (ROI) analysis
   —Warranties

   —Operational description of the equipment or system
   —Deliverables
   —Terms and conditions
   —Management resumes/project-related information
   —Schedules
   —Training
   —Documentation
   —Implementation
   —Options
 7. Glossary/nomenclature
 8. Index
 9. Appendix

## The Cover Letter

The cover letter is your official transmittal message. A formal introduction, it presents your company's offer to your corporate client.

  The cover letter is part of the proposal package and should help sell your solution. It should reference the RFP by name or number and indicate the effective period for the prices and implementation schedules outlined in the proposal. It can also mention the key selling benefit of your proposal.

  The cover letter is also the place to thank individuals in the client's organization who have been helpful to you. Don't gush. Just state clearly and simply that you appreciate So-and-so's help in gathering data, because your analysis and proposal would have been less effective otherwise.

  If your proposal is a revision, indicate that in the cover letter. Let the client know that the proposal has been reconsidered and rewritten to address his or her concerns. You may want to point out specific sections where changes have been made.

  Finally, some proposal writers include a statement of proprietary rights in the cover letter. A brief paragraph of this sort might read:

> This proposal contains confidential and proprietary information. It should not be disclosed to any individual or organization who is not a direct recipient or authorized reviewer of this proposal.

However, a notice like this has a rather negative tone, so you may prefer to put it on a separate page, usually immediately following the title page.

## SAMPLE COVER LETTER 1

[date]

Mr. Samuel Taylor, CPA
Chief Financial Officer
Kallaher Financial Group
123 E. Fourth Street, 5th Floor
Redlands, California

Dear Mr. Taylor:

We are submitting the enclosed proposal in response to your request for the audits of the following hospitals and nursing facilities:

- the Patriot Center for Rehabilitative Medicine in Lodi, California
- the Phoenix City Hospital in Phoenix, Arizona
- the Moreno Valley Wellness Center in Sunnymead, California
- the Claremont Health Care Center in Claremont, California

Our proposal calls for the audits to be handled by a partnership between Thompson/McNeel, a Redlands, California-based firm with extensive experience in real estate audits, and James J. Harrison, CPA, & Company, a firm with offices in Phoenix,

Arizona, with recognized expertise in supporting the health care industry. This partnership is uniquely qualified to handle the audit and provide additional services as may be required.

We believe that we will bring some distinct advantages to the process of handling your audit.

1. As medium-size firms, we have the flexibility and responsiveness to meet all deadlines, especially those imposed by third parties and regulators. We offer you the level of service and commitment that the national firms save for their largest clients.
2. At the same time, we have the resources, specialized knowledge, and experience to handle complex audits of long-term care facilities quickly.
3. Senior partners of both firms will be involved in conducting your audit.
4. We provide the highest quality services at a cost-effective price.

Our proposal addresses your need for thorough audits, but we have also gone a step further. We have developed an overall plan to help you gather the necessary data, make the right decisions, turn the properties around financially, and protect the investment's value.

We believe that it's important to develop an overall picture of the situation in the course of performing this service. In addition, we believe we can offer economies of scale and effort by handling all four audits. For these reasons, our firms would decline to participate in a split or partial award of the audits.

We are eager to work with you on this project.

Sincerely,

Donald Miller, CPA                    Nancy Jamison
Partner                               Manager

## SAMPLE COVER LETTER 2

[date]

Mr. Fred Landers
Director, Professional Development
Canadian Micrometer
155 Lake Louise Drive
Banff, Alberta
Canada

Dear Mr. Landers:

We are submitting the enclosed proposal to provide commercial management training in response to your recent RFP #91-B433. We believe this proposal offers an exceptional range of experience and the depth of resources necessary to meet your training needs cost-effectively.

As the enclosed proposal shows, we specialize in the development of tailored management courses. Each member of the Management Performance, Inc., team is a dynamic presenter, bringing to the classroom both formal training and years of experience in commercial management functions. We have established an outstanding record for tailoring programs to meet the needs of both the client organization and the individual participant.

We also offer you the flexibility of combining various training media. In addition to years of success in developing and presenting classroom instruction, we are experienced in creating self-paced learning materials, interactive and computer-based instruction, and educational videos.

Please note that the enclosed proposal is exactly that: a recommendation based on our preliminary look at your needs. However, to finalize the content of the training and to agree upon the proper medium for the training, we would welcome the opportunity to meet with you. In the process we can become more familiar with your exact requirements.

We look forward to working with Canadian Micrometer and are committed to providing cost effective, top-quality support of your training initiative to increase the skill and knowledge of your professional staff.

Sincerely,

Ursula E. Drew
Manager, Account Development Services

## SAMPLE COVER LETTER 3

[date]

Ms. Mary Carpenter
U.S. Department of Housing and Urban Development
Office of Procurement and Contracts
[address]
Washington, D.C. 20410

Reference: Solicitation No. EV211D1111127204

Dear Ms. Carpenter:

We are pleased to submit the enclosed proposal to provide the research, writing, editing, proofreading, text entry, manuscript preparation, and special services necessary for producing a *Handbook* for the United States Department of Housing and Urban Development.

Documentation Plus, a qualified small business, will serve as prime contractor. As the enclosed proposal shows, we are writers foremost, specializing in legal and technical communications. Each member of the Documentation Plus team has experience writing about legal issues, particularly in the areas of housing and civil rights. In addition, we are familiar with several media, having produced technical journals, magazines, newsletters, newspapers, A/V presentations, videotapes, and film.

American Legal Resource Systems, a minority-owned, qualified 8a small business, will serve as subcontractor on the project. ALRS has extensive experience in providing publications support services to commercial, federal, and other government accounts. These services include technical writing and editing, graphics and production, document design and development, and desktop publishing.

We look forward to working with the Department of Housing and Urban Development and are committed to providing cost-effective, top-quality support of all your writing, editing, graphics, and publication-related needs.

Sincerely,

James. T. Olson
President

## Title Page

The title page should include a title for the proposal, the name of the recipient, the name of the preparer(s), and the date of submission. You can also put the client's logo and your company's logo on the title page. (Be careful of using the client's logo, however; some companies are very touchy about anyone reproducing their logo.)

Some federal programs and some RFPs prepared by consulting organizations specify a format for the title page or even provide a form for you to complete. Use it.

Give your proposal a title. Remember that the title of your proposal may be the first part of it that clients read. Avoid generic titles such as "A Proposal for New American Corporation." That doesn't say anything more than the obvious.

A good title should do the following:

- Describe your recommendation
- Contain an active verb that stresses a benefit to the client
- Focus on results, not product names
- Avoid any use of jargon

An effective way to create a title is to write it in two tiers. The first tier, or main title, describes the benefits and/or results. The second tier links your company with the client. Here's an example:

---

# REDUCING DATA TRANSMISSION COSTS

A Union Technology Solution for AmeriBank Corporation

---

**SAMPLE TITLE PAGE 1**

# Providing High-Quality Management and Supervisory Training Support

## A Proposal From
## Training Specialists International
## to
## the Library of Congress

Submitted in Response to RFP #91-29

date

**SAMPLE TITLE PAGE 2**

# Enhancing Job Performance Through Computer-Based, Self-Paced Training

A Proposal From
Educational Technology, Inc.
to
Patterson Chemicals, Inc.

date

## Table of Contents

One of the key principles of successful proposal writing is to make the proposal easy to use. The table of contents is an effective tool for achieving this goal.

The table of contents should list the titles of each section and the major headings within those sections. It should provide the reader with a sense of the logical structure of the proposal. Numbering sections and subsections can help show the structure, too.

Number pages consecutively through the entire proposal. Don't start renumbering the pages with each section.

**SAMPLE TABLE OF CONTENTS 1**

# *Table of Contents*

## SAMPLE TABLE OF CONTENTS 2

# *Proposal Contents*

1.0 Executive Summary:

Six Benefits of Using Knowlton Technology to Automate Inspection of Turbocharger Assemblies

2.0 Technical Description:

2.1 Functional Description of the Inspection Process

2.2 The Vision System

2.2.1 System Components
2.2.2 Mechanical Description
2.2.3 Electrical Description
2.2.4 System Specifications
Performance Specifications
Applicable Codes and Standards
2.2.5 Ergonomics: User-Friendly Design
2.2.6 Safety
2.2.7 Documentation

3.0 Cost Proposal

## Executive Summary

The executive summary is the single most important part of your proposal. It's the only part of your proposal that's likely to be read by everybody involved in making a decision. In fact, it's the *only* part of your proposal that some decisionmakers may read.

Here are some key guidelines:

1. Write the executive summary so that it is accessible to anyone from the janitor to the chairman of the board.

2. Focus on organizational issues and benefits and keep technical content to the essential minimum.
3. Keep the executive summary short—one to two pages for the first twenty-five pages of proposal text and an additional page for each fifty pages thereafter.

Remember that the last comment regarding length is just a guideline, not an absolute rule. Write an executive summary that tells your story clearly and persuasively, even if that takes an extra page or two.

The structure of the executive summary is almost identical to the structure of the letter proposal. Keep it focused on solving the client's problem. Write it as though it were entitled, "Why My Company Is the Right Choice to Solve Your Business Problem With [Whatever]."

## SAMPLE EXECUTIVE SUMMARY 1

# *Enhancing Communications and Increasing Productivity at North American Chemicals*

## The Opportunity and the Challenge

North American Chemicals' trial application of our competitor's voice mail system has already demonstrated a tremendous opportunity to increase employee productivity and reduce long-distance costs. But any opportunity such as this also contains an inherent challenge: maximizing the potential payoff that the opportunity offers.

In order to gain the greatest possible benefit from the introduction of a voice messaging system, North American Chemicals should consider four key factors:

- *The system's ease of access and user friendliness.* Will employees and customers actually use it?
- *The professionalism of the image the system creates, both for individuals and for the company as a whole.* Does the system enhance the company's image or detract from it?
- *The technical quality of the system.* Is the system technically robust enough to accommodate future needs, adaptations, modifications, or enhancements as North American Chemicals needs them?
- *The overall value of the system.* Will it quickly and conveniently become an everyday tool? Will it be fully supported? Will it fit into the overall telecommunications system?

The challenge for North American is to select the system that offers the biggest payoff in terms of these key factors.

## Ease of Access and User Friendliness

Voice messaging systems are growing rapidly, and the technology behind these systems is evolving rapidly. Other than advances in mass storage systems, most of the enhancements have focused on making the systems easy to access and easy to use. Indeed, the earlier forms of voice mail systems, which started the movement five years ago, now seem like technical dinosaurs: confusing, time-consuming, and difficult to use.

This last is an important factor, because any new service or technology confronts some level of resistance upon its introduction. By choosing the system that offers the shortest available "learning curve," a system that is easy and quick to use, North American will enhance the success of the system. Employees and customers alike will use the system or resist it, depending on how easy it is to understand. If they don't use it, the system obviously won't deliver the full potential of improved productivity.

No system available today has a faster rate of acceptance among users than Vox Populi's voice messaging system. The Vox Populi system is at the leading edge of developments in the vital areas of easy access and user friendliness. That means it will quickly become a widely accepted and appreciated tool within the company and that North American will derive the maximum payoff in terms of efficiency and productivity by choosing it.

## Enhancing Your Professional Image

Since the voice messaging system you select will often be your customer's first contact with North American, it's important to choose a system that offers the highest level of professionalism. After all, first impressions are easier to make than to undo.

The Vox Populi Message Network offers a number of features that will enhance the professional image of North American Chemicals and its employees:

- Single-digit voice prompts that are simple to use. (Other systems sometimes require entering four digits or more.)

- Greetings and instructions that duplicate real human speech. (Many systems do not have access to advanced voice synthesizer technology; as a result, their messages sound artificial and robotic. The overall impression on callers is negative.)
- Designations for messages that are "Urgent" and "Private."
- Guest mailboxes.
- 24-hour support.

## Technology Today: The Issue Is Quality

In selecting your system, therefore, it is important to evaluate how well each potential vendor has kept pace with the technology curve. Will the vendor continue to update the system technically, offering valuable enhancements quickly without disrupting your system's functioning?

The Vox Populi Message Network is a technologically advanced system, positioned to respond to the growing sophistication of voice mail users and the rapid growth of applications and enhancements for this service. As thousands of users can testify, it's easy to use and quickly becomes accepted.

In addition, our products and services in the voice messaging area have expanded rapidly to include not only a service bureau but a full range of premise-based products. Whatever your needs may be now, no matter what they may become as you grow, Vox Populi can support them.

## Overall Value: System, Support, and Service

Vox Populi is unique in its ability to offer North American Chemicals a single source for all of your telecommunications needs. Whether you are looking for on-site equipment, voice messaging services, office automation, or networking services, we can supply the products, services, and expertise to meet your needs. And all the service and support you could ever need are available locally.

Your Vox Populi support team will manage all aspects of your voice messaging system's implementation and will customize the system to ensure that it meets your specific needs. Vox Populi can provide unlimited local training and remote teletraining to familiarize your employees with the system's features and operation. In addition, we schedule regular teletraining broadcasts to provide helpful hints on how to use the system even more effectively.

There's another key benefit from working with Vox Populi for your voice messaging system. Because the system is locally based, it will save you money. Local callers won't need to dial an 800 number for messages. Instead, they can simply dial a local number. This will keep long distance charges associated with using an 800 number to a minimum.

## The Vox Populi Message Network: Advanced Features, Lower Costs

Installing a voice messaging system at North American Chemicals will enhance the productivity and accessibility of your sales team. And it will lower your net long-distance costs.

The key difference is that the Vox Populi Message Network will offer the highest possible payoff. It will give North American Chemicals an easy-to-use service that will be up and running in a minimum amount of time. Your employees and customers will use it eagerly because of its simple, intelligent design and advanced features. And because the Message Network is a technologically advanced offering, positioned to respond to the growing sophistication of voice mail users, it will enhance North American's professionalism and keep pace with your needs.

Choosing Vox Populi's Message Network will maximize the success of voice messaging for North American Chemicals. It will give you the best available tool for communicating with your sales force. And it will give your customers the best available tool for communicating with North American.

When you consider the four key factors of user friendliness, professionalism, technological quality, and overall value, you come to one inescapable conclusion: Vox Populi's Message Network is the best choice for North American Chemicals.

SAMPLE EXECUTIVE SUMMARY 2

# Executive Summary

## Introduction

The Davisson Radiation Laboratory needs to investigate and define the feasibility of a high-radioactivity, multi-axis flexible machining cell in support of its overall mission objective. Such a study, if handled successfully, will position Davisson to proceed efficiently and cost-effectively into the natural next phase, the actual acquisition of such a cell.

But conducting a technical design and cost analysis of such an advanced cell is no easy task. It requires an almost unique combination of experience, technical resources, and commitment to the process of research and development in the machine tool industry. By partnering with a vendor who can supply these qualities, Davisson will receive a workable, practical design that meets all of the required needs and a judicious selection of the desirable features. Further, partnering with such a vendor will help Davisson avoid wasting time and resources because technically inappropriate recommendations will be eliminated from consideration early in the process.

## Why Continental Manufacturing Systems Should Perform This Study

There are three reasons why Continental Manufacturing Systems should perform this study in conjunction with Davisson Radiation Laboratory:

- Continental Manufacturing Systems' expertise, longevity, and resources as a supplier of machine tools, flexible manufacturing system designs, and machining solutions are unparalleled.

- Continental Manufacturing Systems is specifically recommending a team approach to assure rapid, cost-effective, and successful completion of this project.
- Continental Manufacturing Systems has effective quality procedures in place that enhance the success of engineering studies and the machine tools and cells created from them.

**Expertise, longevity, and resources.** Continental Manufacturing Systems is ideally suited to perform this study as a partner with Davisson Radiation Laboratory. The Continental Manufacturing Systems name is synonymous with advanced machining cell design and production. For more than fifty years, Continental Manufacturing Systems had met the world's needs for quality machine tool products and has exceeded customer expectations for quality and performance. This is an important track record for Davisson to consider, because it gives clear evidence of Continental Manufacturing Systems' experience and commitment.

Continental Manufacturing Systems' record of success has resulted in a financially stable company with technical resources that are second to none. In addition, Continental Manufacturing Systems has an extensive research and development division, staffed with leading experts in the fields of machining applications, controls, and design. Whenever specialized machining problems arise, industries and mission-oriented agencies around the world turn to the expertise of Continental Manufacturing Systems.

For this project, it's important to note that Continental Manufacturing Systems has extensive design and manufacturing experience with specialized machining and turning centers. Some of the most advanced work in this area has been performed by Continental Manufacturing Systems, with funding from various commercial and military sources. Continental has designed and built numerous manufacturing systems and cells incorporating advanced material-handling equipment, computers, robots, machine tool equipment, and sensors.

**Team approach.** Continental Manufacturing Systems will use a team approach to complete the engineering study and produce the deliverables called for in Phase I of this activity. The project team will combine the experience and expertise of personnel from both Davisson Radiation Laboratory and Continental's Special

Applications Division. There is no question that this project will benefit significantly by drawing upon Davisson's expertise in high-radiation machining processes.

Continental Manufacturing Systems has successfully provided project management for other projects that benefited from this kind of team approach. Continental will manage and integrate the team so that Davisson has a single point of contact and accountability. Within that framework, the collective expertise, experience, and capabilities of both organizations will be marshaled for maximum effectiveness.

**Quality processes.** Part of the reason for Continental Manufacturing Systems' success has been a long-standing commitment to high-quality products and services. Quality assurance is inherent in Continental Manufacturing Systems' design and production methodologies. This means that Continental Manufacturing Systems will conduct the study using approaches and system structures that ensure clear definitions of Davisson's needs, outline common objectives, and result in a mutually satisfactory design study.

This project will be conducted within the framework of the Continental Manufacturing Systems quality assurance methodology, which includes measurement procedures and an appraisal system to ensure that quality criteria are met for all phases of each project. This process means the project will meet milestone dates on time, stay within budget, and satisfy Davisson's needs.

## Benefits of a Partnership Between Davisson and Continental Manufacturing Systems

By awarding the Phase I contract to Continental Manufacturing Systems, the Davisson Radiation Laboratory will derive a number of vital benefits:

- A cost-effective design that includes a maximum number of the desirable features outlined in the RFP and an optimal mix of the optional features

- Effective project management emphasizing the value of the team approach
  —Cost-effective approaches to conducting the study
  —Unsurpassed technical expertise
  —Quality procedures in all aspects of the project
- A design study that can be easily translated into a Phase II specification

The attached proposal provides detailed substantiation for our recommendation that Davisson choose Continental Manufacturing Systems for the Phase I project. We are eager to work on this project and bring it to a successful conclusion.

## SAMPLE EXECUTIVE SUMMARY 3

*The bottom line is this:*
*MidAmerican Metal Fabrications can improve productivity*
*and increase overall profitability by an additional $5/ton.*

# *Executive Summary*

The American steel industry has become fiercely competitive during the past decade. Given that fact, MidAmerican Metal Fabrications's decision to install a continuous slab caster is a vital step forward. It promises to enhance MidAmerican Metal Fabrications's productivity and profitability. In fact, industry analysts have applauded the move:

> Installation of a $45-million continuous slab caster at Silverman Group's MidAmerican Metal Fabrications plant has analysts bullish on the company's future. . . .

> According to Louis E. Hannen, an analyst with Wheat First Securities Inc. in Richmond, Va., . . . the caster . . . will reduce costs by $30 per ton of steel and increase annual capacity from 300,000 tons to about 500,000 tons. Silverman Group will also be able to produce a higher grade of product and won't have to sell as much lower priced, substandard steel.

> *The Midwestern Business Courier* II:40, p. 2

However, MidAmerican Metal Fabrications must manage the entire process of implementing a continuous caster to make sure it wrings every bit of profit and productivity improvement from the new equipment. And that means not overlooking a vital element in the process: scrap handling.

Unless decisive action is taken quickly, the current scrap-handling system will quickly prove to be a limiting factor, one that reduces the actual payoff from the continuous caster installation.

There are four problems inherent in the current scrap-handling system:

1. The current system limits the number of grades of scrap that can be used in a given blend and does not provide an effective means for controlling the blend.
   - This means that potential opportunities to reduce blending costs will be missed.
   - It also means that there will be inherent inconsistencies in the scrap mix, causing variations in melt chemistries and potential caster interruptions.
   - The current system provides only limited traceability when problems do occur.
2. The current operating system is inefficient and occasionally unreliable.
   - In some instances, scrap must be handled twice for the same operation because of remote storage in Area 17.
   - The current operation cannot handle barge shipments.
   - The current system's unreliability has resulted in melt shop downtime.
3. The current scrap yard is logistically constrained.
   - It offers limited flexibility and places MidAmerican Metal Fabrications at the mercy of scrap market fluctuations.
   - It limits the potential for future expansion.
4. The current yard offers limited capacity, which may result in dangerously low inventory levels once the continuous caster is running.
   - It threatens the full productivity of the new caster system.
   - Responsiveness to customer demands will be hampered without adequate inventory.

SCJ and Company proposes a solution to these scrap-handling problems that will maximize the productivity and profitability of the continuous converter. In addition, our approach to scrap handling will enhance product and process quality. It will eliminate problems with scrap flow, inventory control, and material handling. It will provide greater traceability and product quality than has been possible with the current system.

In the attached proposal we demonstrate the return on investment possible with a change in the method of scrap handling. The bottom line is this: A change in scrap handling now will dramatically improve productivity and increase overall profitability of the MidAmerican Metal Fabrications operation by an additional $5/ton. This system will pay for itself and still deliver additional profits. And note that SCJ and Company is so confident of its ability to provide a technically sound, profitable solution for MidAmerican Metal Fabrications that it is offering you a guarantee. This guarantee is outlined in Section III.

The attached proposal also outlines the technical specifications of the system, showing how scrap would flow through the process and how blending processes would be enhanced. SCJ and Company will provide a range of services: scrap procurement, stockpiling, blending, bucket loading, and delivery to the melt shop. This will enable your melt shop to run at peak productivity and will even open up additional work area because you will be able to remove the cranes currently used in the melt shop to handle scrap. In addition, the system includes a data link between the scrap yard and the melt shop that will provide immediate communications, an on-line status report of the buckets ready for the caster, and permanent record storage for precise traceability.

The move to continuous casting is a necessary next step in the growth of MidAmerican Metal Fabrications's business. It's a vital move to maintain cost competitiveness. But unless that step includes new processes for scrap handling as proposed by SCJ and Company, continuous casting cannot deliver its full payoff to the bottom line: increased productivity, enhanced quality, and greater profitability. We recommend adoption of this proposal now so that the new scrap-handling process can be ready when your continuous caster goes on line.

## Body

The actual "meat" of your proposal goes in the body. What should you address in this section? Here are some suggestions:

- Technical details, design specifications of your recommendation

- Costs and return on investment: the cost justification
- Implementation schedules and issues
- Key personnel who will oversee the project
- Logistical and support issues
- Warranties
- Documentation issues
- Training issues
- Related applications that have been successful
- References to satisfied clients

Not every proposal need address all these issues. Use the RFP as your guide. Also, remember that these elements should be presented in the order of their importance to the decision-maker. If technical competence is not much of an issue, you should address it later in the proposal and deal with those matters of greater concern first.

### Technical Volume

In presenting details and evidence in the proposal body to support your claims, follow these guidelines:

1. Stay focused on the central strategy you established in the Executive Summary.
2. Be objective—don't let your enthusiasm carry you away into using wild superlatives or making unsupported claims or remarks suggesting certainty. Don't project results you're not sure you can deliver. (*Note: This is important. There are legal implications to anything you write in a proposal. If you win the contract, your proposal becomes a legally binding document and you can be held to any claims you have made.*)
3. Use enclosures to support your claims.
4. Mention references, successes, and testimonials.
5. Use specific, concrete language. Simply saying that a system is "efficient" or "ideal for these purposes" is hardly enough. Go into detail. If the readers are interested, they'll read it.

In the technical sections, you may need to describe how equipment or mechanisms work. Try the following outline:

I. Introduction

    A. Define/identify the mechanism

        1. Formal definition, indicating the mechanism's function or purpose

        2. General physical characteristics (including a comparison or analogy to a more familiar object)

        3. Main parts

    B. Indicate why the description is important to the reader

II. Part-by-part description

    A. Part number one

        1. The function or purpose of the part

        2. Physical characteristics (including comparison)

        3. Division into subparts

            a. Subpart number one

                (1) What the subpart is

                (2) Its function or purpose

                (3) Appearance

                (4) Detailed description

                    (a) Shape

                    (b) Size

                    (c) Relationship to other parts

                    (d) Methods of attachment

                    (e) Material

                    (f) Finish

*(Complete the description by going through each part and subpart in order.)*

Don't forget to conclude your description by returning to the selling strategy, showing why this mechanism will help do the job it's intended to do, how it will help solve a problem or meet a need.

    You may also find yourself writing proposals in which you

have to describe processes. For example, if you're asked for a statement of quality control procedures or if you are asked to present a proposed design study, you're being asked to describe a process. Here's a basic outline you can use:

I.  Introduction
    A.  Define/identify the process
        1.  Formal definition: What is the process
        2.  Statement of significance: Why is it done, why does it happen
    B.  Indicate the necessary conditions
        1.  Time and setting: When and where it is done, how it happens
        2.  Personnel: Who performs it
        3.  Equipment: What is needed
    C.  List the key steps

II. The key steps
    A.  Key step number one
        Note: Each step is itself a process. Organize it by following the format above.
    B.  Key step number two, etc.
        Note: The organization of a process description is always chronological; for a cyclical process, simply choose a logical starting point and follow the complete cycle.

In your closing, you might want to comment on the process's significance or indicate its place in a larger scheme of activities. If your process is different from your competitors', you could also mention other methods by which the process can be performed, indicating why you have chosen to do it the way you have. Again, don't forget to "sell" your description. Stress improvement in productivity, cost efficiency, whatever this process can deliver.

## SAMPLE TECHNICAL SECTION

# 2.0 Technical Overview

This section responds specifically to the functional objectives outlined in your RFP. It provides point-by-point confirmation of ComStar's ability to provide the system you want, with those areas requiring customization of the DataMaster platform clearly identified.

Our strategy of using the DataMaster System as a platform for developing American Cellular's EtherSwitch system will enhance the final product in two ways:

First, given ComStar's experience in providing billing and management systems for the cellular marketplace and our resources in developing new systems or customizing existing ones, American Cellular can confidently expect a state-of-the-art solution that will successfully and reliably meet your needs.

Second, because work on the DataMaster platform is well under way and is being underwritten by ComStar, American Cellular will receive a comprehensive, high-quality product at much lower cost than would be possible if the entire system were created as a custom project. We believe it makes good business and technical sense to use DataMaster as the platform for Ether-Switch. Why reinvent the wheel when ComStar already has one that rolls beautifully?

However, using DataMaster as a platform means that we respond in the following pages to your functional needs and pay close attention to your objectives from a business perspective. In some cases, we can offer the same functionality that you specify in the RFP, but because that functionality will be delivered by a system based on our existing platform, the system architecture may not conform exactly to the design specifications you have included in the proposal. These differences will be invisible to the user. However, we do want to be clear that in some instances we deliver the functional requirement but do it in a different part of the system or with a different logical flow of processing steps.

ComStar can produce a system that delivers the functional needs you have specified and that conforms precisely to the design included in your RFP. However, proceeding that way would require much more customization and, in a few instances, would require a completely new development effort. As a consequence, the project would probably take longer and would certainly cost more.

## Cost Volume

Talk convincingly about price. Some RFPs are very detailed in their instructions on presenting cost information; some require cost details in a separate volume; some never mention costs. Regardless of how you handle cost detailing, you should always strive to put cost in the larger context of your solution's return on investment.

Use the following techniques to handle cost and price issues in a natural, effective way:

1. Introduce price only after presenting the solution and its virtues in detail.
2. Don't talk about price in the first or last paragraph of the cover letter or in the executive summary.
3. Whenever possible, mention price in a sentence that also talks about benefits. For example: "The cost for a system that can handle all of your payroll, budgeting, forecasting, and analysis needs is surprisingly low, probably less than $3,000 per month for a company the size of yours."
4. As in the example in (3), try to state price in a complex or compound sentence, putting the actual price in a dependent clause.
5. State the price in terms of small units—$3,000 per month instead of $36,000 per year.
6. If facts are available, use specific figures to show how much time or money the product or service will save; how much more economical it is than competing systems; or how cost-effective it will be in comparison to the system currently being used.

7. Avoid providing detailed pricing on an item-by-item basis. That encourages the detail-oriented to nitpick and makes it easier for unscrupulous clients to shop your proposal to your competitors.

### Calculating Cost/Benefit Ratios and Return on Investment

You may already have an excellent method for calculating return on investment (ROI) potential and for determining the cost/benefit ratio of what you're proposing. If you don't, here's a fairly simple three-step process for providing cost justifications with a credible emphasis on payback and profitability improvement. The point really isn't so much how you do it, but whether or not you do it at all. Too many proposals are sent out with raw pricing data that hasn't been put in the context of overall return. That's a big mistake.

*Step 1.* Calculate the overall investment cost of your proposed solution. Think about elements as the cost of the actual product or service, plus other costs the client may incur, such as costs for installation, training, or required improvements to the physical plant. Then subtract all the costs the client will *avoid* by purchasing your solution. Include such things as repairs, maintenance, and upgrades to what you're replacing. Also, include the cash value to the client of selling or leasing out the old equipment, if that's possible.

*Step 2.* Calculate the annual cost benefit of your proposed solution. You should look at sales revenue, production volume, or other areas of the business operation where your solution will have an impact. Compare what you're proposing with what the client currently has or with what a competing system could provide. Subtract the variable costs involved in the use of your solution compared with what the client has or could get from a competitor. In particular, look at labor, materials, and maintenance. Next, subtract the value of any losses incurred because of system limitations. For example, a machine tool that requires extended downtime for tooling changeovers may have a lower overall productivity rate than one that runs a little slower but that can be changed faster. Total the variable costs, and subtract them from the projected total cost benefit.

Next, subtract any fixed costs the client will incur for your proposed solution and for the current and/or competing solutions. You now have net cost-benefit figures for your proposed system and for what you're going up against.

*Step 3*. Calculate the rate of return on the proposed investment by dividing the net cost benefit into the total investment cost.

## Appendix

The appendix contains supplementary information and attachments. It's not a garbage can into which you should throw everything that might conceivably be of interest. Instead, think of it as the section of the proposal to which the true specialist will turn to get specific, detailed information.

Consider including technical specifications, testimonials, case histories, or research studies in the appendix. You can also include product brochures, annual reports, and capabilities statements for your company and/or any partners.

## Some Final Thoughts

Here are some additional tips that will help you organize your proposal effectively:

1. *When responding to an RFP, respond completely.* Answer every question, no matter how stupid, annoying, or irrelevant it may seem. Do not make perfunctory comments (such as "See above" or "See attached brochure" or "Comply"). Failing to answer or giving perfunctory answers may be seen as nonresponsiveness.

2. *Figure out ways to make your marketing case.* Some RFPs attempt to limit your opportunities to do this. They attempt to limit the content or length of your proposal. If an RFP states

that you may not include any "marketing" or "sales" material or if it specifies that you must answer only the questions in the RFP and nothing else, you can still make your case. Here are some suggestions:

- Turn the cover letter into an executive summary.
- Write each answer as completely and persuasively as possible.
- Use language that suggests the reliability, efficiency, and scope of your solution.

3. *Avoid using boilerplate sections that have been written for other proposals or for generic applications.* They may not work. Rewrite them.

4. *Write technical sections with an eye to organizational impact.* Do not include technical data for its own sake, and do not include any internal technical documentation without thoroughly rewriting it. Technology for its own sake does not persuade.

5. *Avoid banal headings and titles.* Rather than "Technical Section," write "Five High-Productivity Features of Amalgamated's Controllers." Look for strong verbs in your titles and headings, especially verbs that imply a benefit to the client.

6. *Number pages consecutively, avoid overusing tabs and dividers, and provide a table of contents for any proposal longer than five pages.* Make the proposal easy to use.

7. *Use order-of-priority structure in assembling the body of the proposal.* The body will discuss technology, cost justification, implementation issues, project management, training, documentation, and so on—but put those items in their order of importance to the client.

# 13

# Formatting Research Proposals and Proposals for Grants

One of the biggest challenges researchers face is finding an appropriate sponsor to fund their research projects. Writing an effective proposal to win research funds or grant money can be just as challenging as writing a sales proposal for millions of dollars' worth of equipment and services. And the challenge can be met only by writing the proposal as persuasively as possible.

Most of what we've already said about persuasive structure and audience analysis applies to research proposals. However, instead of focusing on profitability or similar business issues, you need to position your proposal to show that it will help the target agency or foundation achieve its mission. In other words, make it clear that your proposed project is fully compatible with the potential sponsor's interests and policies.

As you look for sponsorship, consider the potential sponsor's overall purpose, past or current activities, and program interests for the future. Other questions you should think about include these:

- What broad objectives does this foundation or agency seek to achieve through its sponsorship activities?
- Is it trying to stimulate interest, accelerate progress, address social problems, or develop new knowledge?
- What type of support does it provide (i.e., capital funds,

endowment funds, research grants, educational project support)?

- What size grants does it award?
- Does the agency or institution impose any geographic limitations on its grant activity?

Usually funding is awarded because of the specific research plan and special competence of the individual researcher or the small group of researchers who make the proposal. However, the actual award is usually made to the university, hospital, or other institution within which the research will be conducted, rather than to the individuals. If you work within such an institution, you will probably have to submit any formal proposals seeking external support for research, instructional, or public service programs to the appropriate sponsored programs office for review before you can submit them to the potential sponsoring agency; check with the administration of your institution for specific guidelines. Keep in mind that such a review can be time-consuming. You should allow for it as you schedule your activities to ensure that you get your proposal submitted before the deadline.

There are three main types of external funding:

- *Grants and contracts.* Grants and contracts arise directly from proposals and/or applications prepared by individual researchers. Grants are awarded by government agencies, industry, or private foundations as a result of an unsolicited proposal sent by an investigator who is interested in a basic research project. Contracts are normally awarded as a result of a proposal submitted in response to a bid solicitation or an RFP offered by a federal or state government agency or, in some instances, by a private company. Contracts often have stricter reporting requirements than grants. If you seek a contract, you may find yourself in competition with private enterprise.

Some government agencies award "cooperative agreements," which are similar to grants except that substantial agency involvement is anticipated during the performance of the project.

- *Fellowships (faculty, predoctoral, postdoctoral).* These awards are normally given directly to the individual researcher, bypassing the institutional hierarchy. The fellowship usually pays a specific dollar amount in the form of a stipend. Many private foundations and government agencies offer this type of support, particularly to new or inexperienced investigators.
- *Unrestricted gifts.* Awards of this type, unlike sponsored programs, usually have no reporting requirements of any kind.

## Preparing Your Research Proposal

When you seek external funding, you need to write a clear, convincing, persuasive proposal, because you may be competing for limited funds.

### Initial Contact

Usually an agency or foundation publishes guidelines, an annual report, or some other kind of information document outlining the procedures you should follow in submitting an application for funding. However, you may find it helpful to contact the agency directly to obtain current application forms, to clarify a policy, or to present a project in outline form to see if it's suitable. Some agencies or sponsors prefer this kind of preliminary contact to help reduce the volume of inappropriate proposals they receive. For projects that arouse their interest, agencies may provide suggestions to strengthen the proposal and make it more competitive. Be careful not to make commitments during this stage, particularly budgetary or scheduling commitments.

### Preproposals

Preproposals are informal, preliminary documents. You can submit preproposals to several different sources of support simultaneously.

The preproposal usually contains the following five sections, depending on the project:

1. *Cover Letter.* This should contain:
   a. An introductory paragraph containing the title of the project
   b. A persuasive statement of objectives and intended outcomes
   c. An offer to develop a formal proposal
   d. A description of the unique qualifications of the research team, institution, or both
   e. A final paragraph indicating your willingness to negotiate or discuss further the project's objectives or budget

2. *Statement of Proposed Research.* Include a brief, clearly written description that provides a general understanding of your project. Remember that some of the people who read this description may lack expertise in your field. Keep it simple, focus on basics, and emphasize the probable benefits or positive outcomes of the project.

3. *Resume.* Summarize briefly your relevant biographical data, emphasizing any special experience that qualifies you for the proposed study.

4. *Facilities.* Briefly describe any special capabilities available at your institution that justify conducting the project there. Also indicate the major equipment needed, carefully explaining any unusual needs.

5. *Budget.* Provide a rough estimate of the project's budget. At this stage an itemized budget is not necessary. All the agency or foundation needs to know is what range of costs the project falls into: $5,000 or $50,000 or $500,000.

In summary, your preliminary proposal should be brief (four to ten pages) and easy to understand. It should leave room for negotiation and contain definite plans for follow-up telephone calls or visits.

### Formal Proposals

Most federal and state agencies provide very specific guidelines and application forms that you must follow in submitting your

final proposal. However, some agencies, and private foundations in particular, may not provide an application form or
guidelines regarding format. Although your formal proposal is
obviously a much more structured document than a preliminary proposal, there really isn't just one "right" way to do it.
In fact, it's important to be flexible. Allow the nature and scope
of your proposed sponsored project and the values and interests of the decisionmaker to determine the proper order of the
sections and the appropriate length of your discussions.

Here's a general outline you can use in preparing a formal
proposal if the agency doesn't provide any specific guidelines:

### Proposal Outline

1. Letter of transmittal
2. Cover or title page
3. Table of contents
4. Abstract
5. Overview/statement of problem
6. Body of proposal
   —The need for the project
   —Objectives (benefits) of the project and their significance
   —The proposed project designs or procedures
7. Facilities/location of project
8. Project personnel
9. References/bibliography
10. Budget/budget justification
11. Certifications
12. Appendices

### Letter of Transmittal

The letter of transmittal offically introduces your formal
proposal to the sponsoring organization. Although you might
write it, it is typically signed by a high-ranking official of your
institution, giving the proposal the stamp of authority.

## Cover or Title Page

Federal and state agencies usually provide their own form for this page. If you haven't worked through one before, they can seem hopelessly confusing and cluttered. Have patience, and take your time.

Most private foundations and industrial sponsors do not provide a title page. In such a case, create your own title page, containing the following data:

1. Title of the proposal. Choose the proposal's title carefully. The same principles apply to a research proposal as apply to any other kind of proposal. Try to stress a benefit, or tie your proposal to the institution's mission or goals. Vague, flat, or highly technical titles are seldom persuasive.
2. Request for Proposal or Solicitation number, if any.
3. Name of the institution to which the award will be made.
4. Name of the funding agency to which the proposal is submitted (e.g., the National Science Foundation, the National Institute of Health).
5. Endorsements. The sponsoring agency may require various endorsements on the cover page. The two most commonly requested are the Principal Investigator(s) and the Authorizing Official. For both, include the person's name, title, departmental or official affiliation, and phone number.
6. Other items. These might include the amount requested and the duration and start date of the project.

## Table of Contents

The table of contents usually follows the title page, although it is sometimes preceded by the abstract. The table of contents should not only serve as a convenient navigation tool through the proposal, but should also provide a general outline of the project. Don't break the contents down beyond one or two subheadings. Do include page numbers in the table of contents; number the pages consecutively throughout your proposal, rather than starting over with each section.

### Abstract

The abstract, the equivalent of the executive summary in a sales proposal, is one of the most important parts of the proposal. It states the nature of the project and explains it in general terms geared to individuals who may lack expertise in your field of study. Keep it brief—about 200 to 500 words—and use plain English. A good abstract states in simple sentences what the problem is, how the problem will be solved or studied, and what benefits or positive outcomes will result from the research.

### Overview/Statement of Problem

The overview orients the decisionmaker to the background of the study, discusses the reasons for the study, and presents the conditions leading to the need for the project. It includes an explanation of the specific problem and how it relates to the need. Pertinent references to related research should be included to demonstrate that the researcher has knowledge of all relevant previous work in the field; make clear how the new research will build on that previous work.

### Body of the Proposal

The body should contain the details of the proposed research. Evaluators will be interested in answers to questions such as the following:

- What are you requesting?
- Why is this project needed?
- What is the significance of the project?
- What are the major objectives, and how do they relate to the problem?
- Can these objectives be evaluated?

- What are the procedures of the project?
- What data will be gathered?
- What is your research design?
- What are the technical details?
- How large is the scope of the project?
- What is the time schedule for various phases?
- What will be accomplished?
- What are the expected end results?
- How will you evaluate and disseminate the results?

## Facilities/Location of the Project

In this section, discuss any unique aspects of the available facilities. Is special equipment available? Does the location offer any advantage? Will you subcontract any part of the study?

## Project Personnel

This section should contain the information needed for the evaluators to assess the qualifications and competence of the personnel. A brief description of key personnel and their proposed roles in the project should precede their resumes. Resumes should include:

- Name, title, address, phone number
- Educational background
- Research and professional background
- Publications
- Professional affiliations

## References/Bibliography

This section is a numbered listing of the relevant literature in your research area.

## Budget/Budget Justification

This section lists the anticipated costs of the project. The RFP or application form will call for a statement of the total cost of the project, with a breakdown of costs per year and by category. The following checklist covers most of the items that typically occur in a research budget. However, it may not include every cost a particular research project might incur. Use it as a starting point.

A. Direct costs
  1. Salaries and wages
     a. Professional personnel (faculty, for example)
     b. Senior assistants (exempt staff or postdoctoral students)
     c. Administrative personnel (nonfaculty exempt staff)
     d. Technicians (exempt or nonexempt)
     e. Graduate research assistants
     f. Students
     g. Secretaries (nonexempt staff)
     h. Hourly help (nonexempt staff or students)
     i. Salary increases (for proposals lasting more than one year)

  2. Fringe benefits on all salaries and wages, including hourly help

  3. Equipment
     a. Equipment purchase costs (list items individually)
     b. Equipment installation, if included on bid
     c. Freight, if included on bid

  4. Travel
     a. Domestic
     b. Foreign
     c. Subsistence costs

  5. Materials and supplies
     a. Laboratory supplies
     b. Books, reprints, journals
     c. Chemicals and glassware
     d. Expendable items of equipment (less than two years' useful life)
     e. Office supplies

           f.  Photo duplication, illustration, film
           g.  Printing services not considered part of publications

    6.  Publication costs for page charges in professional journals

    7.  Consultant costs

           a.  Fees, plus travel and lodging expenses

    8.  Computer services

           a.  Central computer system costs
           b.  Departmental uses/maintenance costs

    9.  Subcontracts

           a.  Third-party costs for a portion of the research done outside the institution

   10.  Other costs

           a.  Alterations/construction/renovation costs
           b.  Communications (phone/postage)
           c.  Conference and meeting expenses
           d.  Equipment leasing/rental costs
           e.  Insurance premiums
           f.  Off-site rental of space
           g.  Participant support costs
           h.  Patient care costs (if appropriate)
           i.  Purchase and care of lab animals (if appropriate)
           j.  Recruitment costs
           k.  Royalty/patent costs
           l.  Specialized service facilities

B.  Indirect costs (determined by type of project and on/off-site status)

C.  Cost sharing (if required)

Certifications

Sometimes you may need to include boilerplate statements providing information or certifying compliance with various policies. For example, you might need to provide information such as:

- Your institution's congressional district
- IRS Employer ID number
- Indirect cost rate agreement data
- Tax-exempt status letter
- Institutional financial statement
- Representations and certifications regarding civil rights, affirmative action, and contingent fees

## Appendices

Any supplementary materials, such as papers, reprints, charts, letters of support, course descriptions, or special brochures, should be included here. Remember, however, that reviewers do not usually read appendices. They use them as references to particular sections of the proposal. Never put anything in the appendices that must be read thoroughly. And don't throw material in just to beef up your proposal.

## *Summary*

In summary, make certain that your formal proposal contains these essential elements:

- A clear description of the problem or area of study, including some indication why this problem is an important one to investigate or why the program is important to develop. Try to align the problem/program with the proposed sponsor's mission, objectives, or interests.
- A statement of both why and how the problem or area will be investigated. Proposals often contain detailed technical descriptions of the proposed methodology, with no indication of the significance of the study or project. In a world where external funding is increasingly scarce and competition is growing, it's important to be explicit about the value of the proposed project.
- A summary of the results or outcomes expected. Indicate the impact the results are likely to have on the current body of knowledge, or explain how the project will meet a community need.

# *Part I*

*This section introduces the proposal, describes the project, lays out the work plan and time schedule, and identifies the project principals and their qualifications.*

## Introduction

The proposed project is the development of a second-generation portable glass-pulverizing plant that recycles glass by completely separating on site the glass particles from all wrappers, metal attachments, and nonglass components. The plant and all related apparatus are mounted on a flatbed trailer and towed by truck wherever glass recycling is required. The processed glass may then be used in fabrication of new products.

The project is based on a patented invention that pulverizes materials such as glass bottles, plate glass, and laminated glass, producing a desired particle of clean glass. The recycled product's relative freedom from contamination is important to manufacturers. Current methods and equipment do not remove enough of the metal caps, neckbands, wrappers, and the like to produce a clean product.

The plant's portability offers several significant benefits. Portability means that the plant can be taken wherever glass is most conveniently recycled, reducing transportation costs by eliminating the cost of shipping the glass to be recycled. Such portability also means that each site can arrange for recycling as needed, rather than maintaining a permanent and separate facility. Local communities can get rid of waste glass safely and efficiently. Glass manufacturers can reduce costs by using clean, recycled glass rather than paying for and processing raw materials. For society as a whole, such recycling means that landfill space is not consumed with reusable glass.

The portable facility processes all three types of glass—clear, brown, and green—for market.

DAG, Inc., believes that the process technology may be transferable to other kinds of recycling in addition to glass; an example might be ceramics.

## Project Description

The greatest challenge in producing small glass particles for use as raw material is achieving a clean product. Conventional hammer-mills are unsuitable for this purpose because they crush the metal parts as well as the glass. The hammermills also overheat and require frequent maintenance.

The portable plant based on this invention separates attachments to the source glass—aluminum caps, neckbands, Styrofoam, etc. Bulk glass is loaded into the feed hopper, transported by a feeder belt to a mill, pulverized, screened of nonglass contaminants, and discharged directly into a truck, trailer, or roll-off container for market.

The invention on which this project is based provides [*proprietary description, deleted from the sample but contained in the actual proposal*].

*Mill Components and Functions.* Following are the main components of the pulverizing mill:

[*Components are itemized in bullet points.*]

*Plant Operation.* The pulverizing mill mounts on a flatbed trailer. The hopper (Figure 1) controls the flow of raw material to a conveyor belt, which transports the material to the pulverizing apparatus of a motor-driven mill. The mill deposits the crushed glass on a second conveyor for delivery to the separation unit. Waste is ejected to a bin or caught on the screen for disposal. This unit extracts the pulverized glass and deposits it onto a third conveyor, which transports it to a removable receptacle of the user's choice.

All components are mounted on a standard-size flatbed trailer, which may be towed by a tractor, dump truck, or similar hauling vehicle.

Three capacities are available: a miniplant capable of six to eight tons per hour, a medium-size plant capable of fourteen to sixteen tons per hour, and a maximum-capacity plant processing twenty-four to thirty-two tons per hour.

*Variables.* Changes in the arrangement of components allow for different raw materials and varying particle outputs. Variables include the size of the component elements, their number of sets, the number of elements per set, their rate of rotation, and the size and location of [*proprietary*]. Also, the composition of the [*crushing apparatus*] can vary to accommodate the products being rendered.

## Work Plan and Time Schedule

Glass recycling is widely practiced in the United States, virtually all of it accomplished by hauling the material from collection points to a processing facility. No other portable plant is now in operation, and the authors of this proposal hold a patent-pending certificate (61, 221–378) and a foreign patent number on the process.

The bulk of the grant funds will be used for research and development of a second-generation machine that is more efficient and cheaper to operate, leading to a demonstration model suitable for EPA evaluation.

The work will be supervised by Project Manager Albert P. Gurney and will begin upon receipt of grant funds.

[*Schedule of tasks and target dates for overall completion by February 1993*]

## Experience and Personnel

[*Resumes of the key members of the team*]

# *Part II*

*This section provides the estimates for performing the project. Following the budget sheet is an explanation of each line item.*

## Budget Proposal

| Cost Category | Total | EPA Share | Proposer's Share |
|---|---|---|---|
| Personnel | $10,000 | $ 7,000 | $ 3,000 |
| Travel | 1,200 | 900 | 300 |
| Equipment | 3,000 | 3,000 | |
| Supplies | 1,000 | 500 | 500 |
| Subcontractor | 1,000 | 1,000 | |
| Other | 300 | | 300 |
| Overhead | 5,000 | 4,000 | 1,000 |
| Totals | $21,500 | $16,400 | $ 5,100 |

### *Explanation*

Personnel
- Albert P. Gurney, Project Manager: $5,000 (200 hours @ $25/hr.)
- Tom Richardson: $5,000 (200 hours @ $25/hr.)

Travel
- Pennsylvania to Washington, D.C., to present project to the Environmental Protection Agency: two people, $1,200

Equipment
- Upgrade motors on the plant to process a higher rate of glass: $3,000

Consumable Supplies
- Maintenance Supplies: $200
- Paper and Office Supplies: $500
- Oils and Grease: $300

Subcontractor
- Engineering Associates: $1,000

Other
- Telephone: $100
- Photocopying: $20
- Videotaping: $180

Overhead
- Estimated Overhead: $5,000

# 14

# Automating the Process

You can build an effective, automated proposal system using nothing more than common word-processing tools, greatly enhancing your productivity. You don't need anything too fancy. In fact, a basic desktop-publishing setup can supply the desired professional look and can also help you create and manage proposals using a customer-driven data base of boiler-plate write-ups.

But should you use boilerplate? Aren't there problems with it? Indeed there are.

Some of the problems with boilerplate are that it's too technical, too detailed, too lengthy, and too intimidating for some readers. Using boilerplate may send the proposal evaluators some negative messages:

- It suggests that you don't care enough about this client and this RFP to do anything more than insert filler and off-the-shelf information in your response.

- It creates a false sense of security for you. Often boiler-plate does not directly address the customer's specific concerns, particularly the business issues, but using it may convince you that you're being responsive when you're not.

- It often focuses attention on the product, service, or vendor, not on the client.

- It may not be focused on your winning strategy.

So how can you use boilerplate? Won't it make your proposals sound canned, stiff, nonresponsive? No, not necessarily.

If you look at the various parts of a formal proposal, you

can see that there are only a few that probably need to be written from scratch each time. The cover letter needs to be tailored, and the executive summary needs to be fresh, although both could contain a paragraph or two that are generic. Most of the other sections, however, can be based on prewritten materials. If you set it up correctly, they'll never look or sound prewritten.

Types of information that can be prewritten and stored in a "boilerplate data base" include:

1. Terms and conditions
   —Domestic
   —International
   —Product specific exceptions
2. Management resumes
3. Training plans
4. Documentation standards
5. Installation plans, matrices, and schedules
6. Case studies and examples of successful previous projects
7. Quality plans and methods

You can also store descriptive information about specific products and services in a data base, with different write-ups emphasizing marketing strategies (quality, technology, cost) and appealing to certain types of decisionmakers (for example, analytical, pragmatic). Specific product features or options can be created as separate files that you can cut and paste, depending on the configuration you're quoting.

You might be able to obtain boilerplate from the following sources:

- Product/service brochures
- Technical product descriptions
- Test or performance reports
- Maintenance and service descriptions
- Visuals and graphics
- Project management descriptions
- Individual resumes

- Annual reports
- Previous proposals

I've helped several clients set up proposal generators, using nothing more complicated than a personal computer, a word-processing system, and a few macros. In truth, the system isn't as important as the files of information you're accessing when you build the proposals.

# 15

# Dressing Your Proposals for Success

I first heard the motto "the package is part of the product" at Procter & Gamble, where they take it very seriously. P&G spends a lot of time and money designing packaging that's durable, attractive, easy to ship, visually appealing, and whatever else a good consumer package should be. And most of us in the past decade have at least glanced at the various "dress for success" prescriptions offered by experts like John Molloy. Although we all believe inner substance is more important than outer appearance, we also know that first impressions are incredibly powerful.

As proposal writers, we can learn from these examples. What we write should be packaged so that it's easy to read and easy to use. What this requires is paying attention to organization and appearance.

Here are ten tips on dressing your proposals for success:

1. *Give each proposal and each section of the proposal a title or subject line to help readers orient themselves quickly.* This is useful even for letter proposals. A substantive title helps readers identify whether this document pertains to them. It also makes the document look a little more professional. Avoid banal or meaningless titles, such as "Proposal," "Technical Section," or "Results." These do nothing more than state the obvious. If possible, express the key point of the proposal or section in the title.

2. *Keep your paragraphs short.* Long blocks of single-spaced type are intimidating to the eye. Whenever you see a long

paragraph, see if you can break it up into two or more short ones. I vividly remember my sophomore English teacher, Percy Totheroh, teaching us that every paragraph must have five sentences: a topic sentence, a restatement, two examples, and a transition or summary. Sorry, Percy. Not true. A paragraph simply covers one topic, with the substantiation necessary to develop that topic. Some topics don't require any substantiation. Therefore, some paragraphs may consist of just one sentence.

3. *Use a clean, legible typeface, and print the proposal on a letter-quality or laser printer*. Avoid producing copy on dot matrix printers unless it's just a rough draft. Also, never include faxes or weak photocopies, and don't include photocopies of manuals, diagrams, or other technical documentation just because it's available.

4. *Use upper- and lower-case letters*. Never use all capitals, except for titles or brief headings. Text printed in capitals is much harder to read and psychologically may make the reader feel as if someone is shouting at him or her.

5. *Use lots of headings and subheadings, even in letter proposals*. Center the main ones, and line the others up along the left margin. Print the subheadings in upper- and lower-case letters and put them in boldface type or underline them.

6. *Don't justify the right margin of your proposal*. Allow it to run unevenly, at natural line lengths. There are three reasons for not justifying text. First, justifying the text makes your document look formal, even institutional, which is probably not what you want. Most people respond more positively to a document that appears at least slightly personal. Second, unless your computer offers proportional spacing and global hyphenation, your text will probably be riddled with odd, uneven spaces among the words, which disrupt the reading process. Third, studies have shown that people read more accurately when text is printed in "ragged right" format, particularly for long lines of text.

7. *Leave ample white space*—generous margins on both sides and room at the top and bottom. Don't make the page look crowded.

8. *Put charts and other tabulated data into the text of your proposal so that the reader doesn't have to rummage around at the back or in the appendix to find them.* Also, print charts and tables in the same orientation as the text. Don't make the reader twist your proposal sideways to look at its charts or diagrams. It's better to simplify or reduce wide layouts if you can rather than running them sideways.

9. *Number the pages consecutively.* Sometimes people start the page numbers over with each new section. If you've ever sat through a proposal review conference where people were trying to look up information in a proposal that's been organized that way, you know what a nuisance it is. Numbering the pages consecutively makes the information easier to identify and locate.

10. *Highlight your key points.* Use every device at your command to make the important stuff jump out: boldface type, underlining, italics, color, bullet points, indentations, boxes, graphics, and anything else. The more highlighting you do, the more likely it is that the decisionmaker will get your key points.

Following these tips won't guarantee that your document will win any "best dressed" awards, but readers will probably find it a lot easier to use than if you just hand them wall-to-wall words.

## Looking Organized Even When You're Not

What makes sense to one person may be incomprehensible to another. But you can certainly make the job of understanding your writing easier for your readers if you pay some attention to basic organization. In fact, anything you write will benefit if you follow three basic principles:

1. Provide an overview of the content and structure of the proposal at the outset.
   —Each section should have some kind of overview (in

addition to the executive summary, which serves that
function for the proposal as a whole).
—Overviews summarize content, focus the reader's
attention, and describe a document's organization.
—Overviews should tell a reader at a glance the key
point of the section and the key results or recommendations. They help you get right to the point.
2. Choose an appropriate pattern for organizing the body
of the document.
—As a general rule, keep the organizational pattern as
simple as possible. Avoid using a chronological structure. Instead present the key point first from the
reader's point of view.
—If you have a lot of detailed information to provide,
break it up into layers, with seven or fewer items in
each layer.
3. Make the organizational pattern visible to the reader.
—Write informative headings—that is, headings that
make substantive statements about the content of the
section they introduce. Rather than heading a section
of your proposal "Recommendations," why not call
it "Three Ways to Solve the Data Base Problem"?
—Provide a clear, functional table of contents.
—Make the proposal easy to skim by highlighting key
points, putting lists in bulleted format, and so on.

These are pretty easy tricks. You don't have to be an Ernest
Hemingway or a Joyce Carol Oates to apply them. But if you
use them, the things you write will look and read a lot better
than if you don't. In fact, they'll look so good that some of
your readers won't notice those rare occasions when you're
not very well organized.

## Design Considerations for Your Proposal

Traditionally, technical proposals had no real design. They
were simply typed, with charts and graphs inserted at the end.
Some proposal writers have actually been hostile toward design
as an element of their document.

But design elements cannot be avoided. Neglect of design is a design decision. Although visual appearance is probably the least important element of a successful proposal, it is nevertheless an element. The way the proposal is packaged is, in fact, part of the overall product. Regardless of content, some documents are more attractive, more professional-looking, more "readable" than others. Some typefaces are more readable and visually appealing than others. Some headings and ways of handling body copy are more likely to "grab" the reader. These differences are elements of design. Good design can help attract attention and establish recognition. It can reinforce the key selling points. And it can subtly imply quality and excellence.

The key design decisions are:

1. Design of page layout
2. Choice of typeface
3. Use of graphics

Here are some specific suggestions on design:

1. Print your proposals on good-quality, bond paper. The paper should be opaque enough that printing won't show through.
2. Proposals of fewer than one hundred pages should be printed on one side of the paper only.
3. Proposals longer than one hundred pages may be printed on both sides.
4. The font should be chosen from the more classic styles: Times Roman, Century Schoolbook, or Palatino, for example.
5. Print your proposals on a laser printer for clarity and crispness.
6. Number pages consecutively within an individual volume.

## Using Graphic Elements

Graphics—charts, diagrams, trend curves, line drawings, and flow charts—can be tremendous aids to communicating effectively. For some readers, graphics communicate more clearly than words. And they improve the overall design of the proposal because they break up the text and stimulate the reader's interest.

Look for opportunities to explain things visually. Here are some guidelines for selecting visuals:

1. Use appropriate visuals—don't include them just because they're available.
2. Avoid highly technical visuals.
   —Use a minimum of complex, technical, or scientific drawings.
   —When you must include schematics, architectural drawings, or similarly technical visuals, place them in technical appendices or attachments.
3. Think about the best places to use graphics as you develop your initial outline, rather than waiting until you've written the entire text.
4. Orient your graphics horizontally on the page.
5. Write active captions for your graphics, and make sure that they stress a customer benefit.
6. Keep visuals simple. Don't try to make more than one point in a visual, and make sure that the key point is clear.
7. Number visuals sequentially.
8. Introduce visuals in the text before displaying them, but try to position them as close as possible to the point in the proposal where they're being discussed.

# Section IV

# Writing to Win

# 16

# Give the Reader a KISS!

Simplify. Simplify. Simplify.

*—Thoreau*

If you ask people what kind of business writing they like to receive, most of them will say, "Gimme a KISS!" That is, Keep It Short and Simple.

Unfortunately, when those same people sit down to write, they too often produce lengthy, verbose, and complicated documents. Especially when writing proposals, they subscribe to the "bulk" theory: Pile on the paper and the reader will give in out of sheer exhaustion. Now, admittedly, there has to be some measure of proportion in your proposals. If you're bidding on a $10-billion job, a letter and a brochure just won't do. But the reason it won't do is that, by its very nature, a job of that size involves a great deal of complexity that needs to be addressed—as succinctly and simply as possible.

Lots of people pay lip service to short, direct, clear writing, but the reality is you won't see much of it. There seems to be a cultural bias against clarity and simplicity. In fact, some children were even taught in school that "good" writing is synonymous with big words, complicated sentences, and convoluted thinking. (Remember? Every week you had to memorize ten big, impressive words, learn to pronounce and spell them, and use them in your theme.) Even today there are books about developing a "power vocabulary," which basically means writing with big words.

People write obscurely out of fear or anxiety or ignorance. But most of us like to receive short and simple communications. Applying the Golden Rule, we should therefore try to send similar communications to others. Because of the importance of making the decisionmaker feel comfortable with your proposal, you should try to write as sparely and economically as possible.

All things being equal, a short, clear proposal is more persuasive than a long, densely worded one. Because your proposal is brief, it's more likely to be read first. That's to your advantage, because it means that your offering establishes the baseline against which others are judged. Because your proposal is easy to understand—because it's readable—it will seem more logical than other proposals.

Here are some tips for using the KISS principle in your proposals:

1. *GYST.* Don't write anything until you "Get Your Stuff Together." Lots of gas-filled balloons are launched from word processors by people who began to write before they really knew what they were talking about, why they were talking about it, or to whom they were talking. Analyze the client's business problem or need, take the time to storyboard your response, and give lots of thought to the decisionmaker's priorities before you commit yourself to an organizational pattern.

2. *Watch your words.* Churchill once said, "Short words are the best words, and old words, when they are short, are the best words of all." Great advice. Whenever possible, use everyday language in your writing. A long, long time ago, Hippocrates, the father of medicine, said, "Clarity is the chief virtue of language, and nothing detracts from it so much as the use of unfamiliar words." What a pity that so few of his latter-day disciples follow his advice.

As a rule, choose one- or two-syllable words. In fact, use them abut 90 percent of the time. Can you still write a powerful message using such commonplace words? Well, one of Lincoln's greatest speeches was his Second Inaugural Address. Of its 701 words, 627 have just one or two syllables. (That's 89.5 percent.)

3. *Use short sentences.* A sentence is an idea. Sentences work best when they contain only one idea. And they work even better when they're short and simple. Try to keep your average sentence length to between seventeen and twenty words. This is one place where less is truly more. Also, limit the number of qualifications and subordinate clauses your sentences contain.

4. *Use a natural tone.* Write in a natural, conversational rhythm to the extent possible. When you go over your proposal, read it out loud. Is it easy to read? Does it flow smoothly, or do you find yourself stumbling over particular phrases or passages? Ask yourself: If I were sitting in front of the decision-maker, how would I say this? Say it. Then write it that way.

Don't think writing short, simple proposals will be easy. You're surrounded by bad examples, and you've probably seen plenty in the RFPs you've read. Writing simply and concisely takes a lot more effort and skill than rambling on does. As the French mathematician Pascal once wrote to a friend, "I apologize for writing such a long letter. I didn't have the time to write you a short one."

But the effort is worth it. In fact, if your proposals embody the KISS principle, your readers may be so pleased they might want to give you a kiss in return. Or even a contract!

# *17*

# Word Choice: Four Traps to Avoid

In their effort to be impressive and to sound knowledgeable, writers often fall into a number of verbal traps. Here are some common ones to avoid.

## Trap 1: Using Jargon

Do you remember how you felt your first few days on the job? A little bit scared? Eager to do well? Confused?

You probably had the experience of hearing people use language that was completely meaningless to you. Or maybe you read memos, letters, or reports that contained lengthy sections of utter incomprehensibility. You were encountering the company's jargon for the first time. And since you were uninitiated in its mysteries, you didn't understand it.

Most people have one of three reactions to these experiences:

- They feel demoralized and wonder if they're unprepared to handle the job competently.
- They become angry at the speaker or writer for failing to communicate in appropriately clear language.
- They question the speaker's competence, wondering whether marginal ability has been hidden behind a thick cloud of technical and pseudotechnical vocabulary.

Obviously, none of these are positive reactions.

But gradually, as you attended more meetings and read more memos, you began to absorb some of the meanings and connotations of the jargon you encountered. Maybe you found a colleague who would define the jargon for you without making you feel like an imbecile. Somehow, almost imperceptibly, what had been unknown and confusing became familiar and comforting. *Their* jargon became *your* jargon. You had successfully completed one of the most important processes of socialization—acquiring the group's language. Instead of being a barrier that kept you out, jargon had become a useful tool which proved you were "in."

And that's when jargon became particularly dangerous for you as a proposal writer. When you can no longer recognize jargon for what it is—the specialized technical language of a particular company, department, industry, or field of expertise—you are most likely to misuse it. Sadly, some people actually seem to lose the ability to communicate in simple, ordinary language. They can't explain to their spouse or kids what they do at work because they can't remember the everyday words to use.

Don't miss the point here: Jargon serves a useful function when it concisely and precisely names something that would otherwise take a lot more words and involve a lot more ambiguity. But it doesn't work if it's not understood by everybody in the intended audience. And when you're writing a proposal, you can assume that at least part of the audience will not understand the jargon.

Obviously, you need to exercise some judgment and common sense. But if you're looking for a general rule on jargon, here's one: *If in doubt, leave it out.*

## Trap 2: Dangling Your Participles and Other Embarrassments

When I was teaching English at UCLA, one of the students in my composition class submitted a paper in which he asserted:

"After molding in the cellar for weeks, my brother brought up the oranges."

I had a hunch I knew what he really meant to say, but in Southern California one never knows. So I wrote in the margin of his paper: "Please do not allow your brother to visit this campus."

What my student had created was, in grammatical terms, a dangling participle; in human terms, it was an embarrassment. *Using dangling participial modifiers* is one of the most common and amusing mistakes people make when writing. Other howlers include *squinting modifiers* and *misplaced adverbial modifiers*.

It's easy to create these things. Everybody who writes occasionally produces one. That's why everyone has to edit. But understanding them can help keep you from creating them as frequently as you might. And it can prevent you from embarrassing yourself in your proposals and undercutting your credibility and professionalism.

### *Dangling Participles*

The most egregious of these constructions is the participial phrase that introduces a sentence. Whatever that phrase modifies has to follow immediately upon it, because that's how the reader's brain will decode it. For example:

> Featuring plug-in circuit boards, this computer offers maximum flexibility and growth potential.

That one's okay. The participial phrase "Featuring plug-in circuit boards" explains something about "this computer," and the noun "computer" immediately follows the phrase. So it's clear, it's unambiguous. It works.

But consider this one:

> Featuring plug-in circuit boards, we can strongly endorse the computer's flexibility and growth potential.

What do we have here? A cyborg proposal writer?

We can fix this one by rewriting it: "Because the computer features plug-in circuit boards, we can strongly recommend it for flexibility and growth potential."

Here's another one:

> Being made of high-strength ceramics, the engineers
> believe the system will last a long time.

We're hiring ceramic engineers now?

### Squinting Modifiers

A different kind of problem arises when you position a modifying word or phrase so that it could modify either of two different elements in a sentence. For example:

> Clients who process data after hours frequently will
> need to use the batch mode option.

"Frequently" is squinting between two parts of the sentence, either of which it could modify. You could be saying that people who make a habit of processing data after hours will have to use the batch mode. Or you could be saying that even one instance of after-hours processing will usually be grounds for using the batch mode.

The sentence should be rewritten to clear up the ambiguity:

> Clients who frequently process data after hours will
> need to use the batch mode option.

Or:

> Frequently, clients who process data after hours will
> need to use the batch mode option.

### Misplaced Adverbial Modifiers

This last construction is hard to describe but easy to demonstrate. You see them in job titles occasionally. For example, a company in my city employs several people as "Vibrating Structures Engineers." The local university refers to one of the

young women in its employ as a "Dishonored Check Collector." It's hard not to feel sorry for these people, isn't it? Perhaps
appropriate medication would help those vibrating engineers,
but probably nothing but time will heal the check collector's
sense of shame.

Be careful when lumping words together to form job titles,
project names, or product descriptions so that you don't provoke unintended laughter.

## Trap 3: Creating Noun Clusters

Within our lifetime, the English language, and particularly that
version of it spoken in the United States, has changed in many
ways. Some of these changes have been for the better: For
example, people no longer say "I shall" and "you or he will"
for future tense. Now, all of us "will" and we leave "shall" to
imply obligation. That's cleaner than the old rule, which never
made much sense anyway.

But some of the changes haven't really improved the
language. In fact, some of them have actually made it much
more difficult for us to understand each other. One of these
changes for the worse is the introduction of what I call "noun
clusters" into written and, occasionally, spoken English.

I call these constructions "noun clusters," but they don't
have an official name yet. If you check your kids' grammar
textbooks, you probably won't find them mentioned. That's
because they're a relatively new phenomenon. Other writers
have called them "jammed modifiers" or have referred to these
constructions as "noun stacking" or "nominalization." But I
call them noun clusters because that's what they are: a cluster
of nouns all wadded together, a bolus of incomprehensibility.

To form a noun cluster, you simply string together a bunch
of nouns. That's it. There's no special talent required for this
activity. In fact, it probably helps to have no talent, or at least
no ear, for language.

You see noun clusters very frequently in technical proposals and technical documentation, but because we all like to
sound smart and high-tech, they're spreading into more mun-

dane areas as well. We frequently see them in job titles, department designations, and those clever names sometimes given to computer applications, names specially chosen so that they form a nifty acronym. And you'll probably see them more often in the title of technical proposals than any other single location.

Bear in mind, it's always been legal in English to use one noun to modify another noun. The first noun functions as an adjective in such a construction and is usually called an "attributive noun." Examples are *telephone company, cellular phone, bus stop, marriage certificate,* and *grocery store.* The problem arises when a whole slew of nouns are crammed together. The poor reader's brain has no way of decoding this mess until he or she has already gone through it once. Then the reader must go back over it, figure out which nouns are functioning as nouns, which are adjectives, and what goes with what, and try to make sense out of it.

Here's a title that appeared on a proposal I received:

FAX TRANSMISSION NETWORK ACCESS COST
OPTIMIZATION PROPOSAL

Or consider these abominable, yet typical, noun clusters from text sections:

It is a direct drive remote terminal software modification package designed by our internal software applications development management group.

Personnel development in our company is guided by an employee testing training development program.

If you catch yourself writing one of these things, what should you do? First, identify the key noun in the sequence. In the first example, there's no verb at all in the title. What is the writer trying to say? That we can "optimize" the costs of accessing network service for transmitting faxes? Maybe. Your guess is as good as mine. But let's assume that's the message. Instead of using a buzzword like "optimize," let's try some ordinary English:

Reducing the Costs of Accessing the Network for Fax
Transmissions

Take a look at the second example. How can that pretzel be
straightened out? First, try to figure out the key action, if any.
In this case, the key action is "designed," although that's not
being used as the main verb of the sentence. "Is" fills that role.

What performs that key action? In this case, it's the "development group." Put that noun up front:

Our development group has designed . . .

Now try to rearrange the remaining nouns in short phrases,
using prepositions to show linkage and converting some of the
nouns to participles:

Our development group has designed a modification
package for software used on direct drive terminals
in remote locations.

That's a little better, isn't it? A little easier to understand the
first time through? The final phrase is still awkward, but the
whole sentence begins to resemble English rather than some
weird technospeak.

Avoid noun clusters in your proposals. They're difficult to
understand, they slow down the reading process, and they
sound awful.

## Trap 4: Using Knotty Words Incorrectly

There are lots of confusing words in English. Some look like
other words but mean something different. Or they can be
correct in one context but not in another. Using these difficult
or "knotty" words incorrectly can diminish your credibility and
even distract the reader. (Of course it's always possible that the
evaluator won't know how to use them correctly, either, and
from the evidence contained in a lot of the RFPs, that's probably a reasonably safe bet. However, it's not worth taking the
chance.)

I remember reading a cover letter recently that stated how much the RFP had "peaked" the writers' interest. Hmm. I don't think so. It probably didn't "peek," either. Maybe what they were trying to say was that the RFP had "piqued" their interest.

Another proposal writer slipped into the common mistake of using a currently popular buzzword in his writing without really knowing what it means. He wrote: "This application is ideal for use in a nitch market." *Nitch*? Have you ever seen a "nitch market"? Do you think one could buy a nitch on sale there?

Okay, I admit it can be confusing. Both of those words come from foreign languages and are spelled in unusual ways. But the mistakes are still bad enough to provoke groans from most educated readers.

So what's a proposal writer to do? Use a dictionary, for one thing. Whenever you're not sure about a word, check it in a good (i.e., hardbound) dictionary. This is especially a good idea if you've been rummaging through the thesaurus looking for nifty new words. Check their meaning before you use them. *Stubborn, obdurate, pig-headed,* and *firm-principled* are all listed as synonyms in the thesaurus, but they don't mean the same thing. (The boss is firm-principled. The jerk two cubicles over is pig-headed.)

Here are some knotty usage problems that can pop up in proposal writing. Maybe a few of them bother you.

*Affect/Effect*   This pair drives people nuts. *Affect* is usually a verb: "Your choice of a motorized log splitter will inevitably affect the logging camp's productivity." *Effect* is usually a noun. "You choice will also have an effect on safety." One way to remember which is which: Think of *"the effect."* "The" can't precede a verb, so link the "e" at the end of "the" with the "e" that begins "effect." (Sometimes people who speak in psychobabble use "affect" to refer to a person's emotional state. And sometimes lawyers like to use "effect" or "effectuate" as a verb, meaning "to bring about or execute." Ignore these people. Nobody ever learned to write clearly by imitating lawyers' or psychologists' styles.)

*Assure/Ensure/Insure*   All three of these words mean about the same thing: "to make certain or secure." *Assure* refers to people, though, and suggests putting someone at ease, reducing anxiety or worry. *Ensure* and *insure* both mean "to secure from harm," but *insure* has a stronger implication. If you *insure* something, the reader may take that as your guarantee of a positive outcome, whereas *ensuring* or *assuring* may imply serious effort on your part but no guarantee.

*Compliment/Complement*   Have you ever seen a menu that promised an appetizer or salad that would "compliment" your meal? But when you ordered it, what happened? Nothing. It didn't say a word. No compliments. No pleasantries at all. *Compliment* means "flattery" or "praise." A *conplement* is something that completes a whole: "The program modules complement each other."

*Data is/Data are*   Everybody who took Latin in high school, and even a few former altar boys, love to pounce on your throat if you say, "The data is in the computer" or whatever. "Data," they snootily inform you, "is the plural form of datum. Therefore, it must take a plural verb." Yeah, well. . . . Maybe that's why Latin is a dead language. Those Romans were too uptight about these things. In fact, *data* as used in English is a "collective singular noun," which is grammar jargon that means it's the same kind of word as *jury, committee, staff,* and *humanity.* If the data you're writing about is a homogeneous whole, use a singular verb: "The billing data is available on tape." But if the data in question is a hodgepodge, use a plural: "Their business and technical data were located in different parts of the system."

*Imply/Infer*   Inference is a mental process. You *infer* something when you reach a conclusion on the basis of observations. Only people can infer: "The client inferred from our documentation that system training would proceed quickly." Implication is a state of being. Data of any kind, including people, can imply things: "The disheveled condition of my desk implies that I am a slob. The look on your faces implies that you are not."

*Incent*   Management has been using incentives for years to motivate employees. But what genius decided to create a new verb by backing *incent* out of incentive?

This is a weird word, one you won't find in any dictionary. It sounds like *incite*, as in riots. It also sounds a little like *incense*, as in infuriate. Here's some advice: Don't use incent as a verb, or you may so incense your readers that you incite them to throw away your proposal.

*Interface* Computer systems, hardware, mechanical parts all *interface*. That's fine, although *connect* or *link* might sound less pompous. But people don't. It sounds ludicrous to say, "Our technical team will interface with your project management team." Today, you cannot be too careful about interfacing with others.

*It's/Its* [also, *who's/whose*]  One of these is a contraction, one is a possessive pronoun. The contraction is the one that has an apostrophe in it. It's a shortened version of *it is*. I think the confusion arises from the fact that in English we form possessives with nouns by adding '*s*, as in John's coat, the chair's padding. But we don't use the apostrophe when forming a possessive from a pronoun: *ours, yours, hers, theirs, its,* and *whose*. Why? Don't ask. It's a tale of greed, stupidity, and squalor that has been an embarrassment to grammarians for hundreds of years.

*Lay/Lie; Raise/Rise; Set/Sit*  These are about as knotty as words get. People make mistakes with them all the time, and usually their readers or listeners aren't certain what's correct, either. The second of each pair, the ones with an *i*-sound, are all intransitive verbs. Big help, right? That means they do not take an object. Each of them is something you do to yourself: "You lie on the couch. You rise for dinner. You sit at the table." (Or somebody else does these things to himself or herself: "She lies on the beach. They rise from their pew. He sits on the board of directors.") The first of each pair are transitive verbs, meaning they are actions performed on something else: "I lay the book on the table. They raise orchids. She set the bags of fertilizer on the driveway." Good luck.

*Oral/Verbal*  *Oral* means with your mouth; *verbal* means with words. Spoken language is oral. Both written and spoken language are verbal (unless you write in hieroglyphics or ideograms). A verbal contract could be either spoken or written. An oral contract is spoken only.

*Parameters*   This word means a variable or a constant in a mathematical expression. (If you have a system characterized by a number of variables and you hold them all constant except one, you will obtain parametric data for that one variable.) Fine. So if you're writing about parameters in that sense, go to it. But if you're using the word because it sounds kind of high-tech and you're using it very loosely to mean "boundary" or "limit," shame on you. You're thinking of *perimeter*, a different word entirely.

*Principal/Principle*   This pair of words is demonstrable evidence that the people who invented English had a shocking lack of imagination. Why have two words that are pronounced exactly the same and which differ only minutely in spelling, and yet which mean totally different things? Maybe it was laziness. Anyway, most of us recall from grade school that "the principal is my pal." (At least until you were sent to his or her office, that is.) But *principal* also means the money on which you're earning or paying interest and means any head person—the principal partner in an accounting office, for example. *Principle* means an axiom, a basic truth, a belief. "Some principal partners have no principles."

*Simple/Simplistic*   Don't write in your proposal that your solution is "simplistic." That's no compliment. *Simplistic* means shallow, and simplistic solutions ignore the complexities of reality. However, writing or speaking simply is a good idea. *Simple*, among other things, means uncomplicated, direct, free of clutter. And that's good. In fact, that's very good in a proposal.

# 18

# Sentence Structure: Maximizing Your Clarity

Lousy proposals have a few characteristics in common. They're product-focused, rather than client-focused. They're disorganized. They're not convincing. And they use pompous language to impress or intimidate their readers rather than to communicate clearly.

This is a sad situation. Even worse, it appears to be contagious. The more you're exposed to this kind of gobbledygook, the more you tend to mimic it in your own writing. Often, the RFPs you receive will be written so badly that it's hard to figure out what they mean. The professional journals you read may contain articles so dense that even the authors may not know what they mean.

I often ask participants in proposal writing seminars to complete lists of the things they like to see in documents of any kind and the things they hate to see. Usually one of the very first positive points people write down is something like "gets right to the point" or "clear" or "easy to understand." Conversely, the negative list almost always includes "vague," "wordy," or "no clear purpose."

Assuming that you subscribe to the linguistic version of the Golden Rule, "Send unto others what you would like to receive yourself," the question arises: How can you write proposals that get right to the point, that are clear, and that are easy to understand?

Here are four techniques you can use to maximize your clarity. (Or just to avoid writing proposals that sound like they were authored by a pompous donkey.)

1. Avoid writing long or overly complicated sentences.
2. Avoid using the passive voice too much.
3. Put your key points in the most prominent position.
4. Make sure you follow Sant's Law in each sentence you write.

Let's take a look at each technique in more detail.

1. *Avoid complicated sentences.* Sentence complexity is a function of two elements: length and syntactic structure. Keep your sentences short. Strive for an average sentence length of from seventeen to twenty words for maximum readability. And try to keep sentences as uncluttered as possible. A sentence is simply an idea. Filling it up with qualifications, parenthetical comments, subordinate clauses, and other rhetorical baggage usually makes it harder to understand.

2. *Avoid the passive voice.* In English you have two options for creating declarative sentences (that is, sentences that make a statement): the active or the passive voice. In the active voice, which we use the vast majority of the time, the grammatical subject does the action. For example:

Our sales team visited the client's headquarters.

"Sales team" is the subject. And they're the ones who did the visiting.

To say the same thing in the passive voice, invert the typical relationship between subject and verb. In the passive voice, the subject receives the action:

The client's headquarters was visited by our sales team.

This sentence is perfectly legal. The grammar police would pass it without any problem. And if you want to focus on what got visited, rather than who did the visiting, it's a good choice.

The problem is that in bureaucratic writing, almost all of the sentences are in the passive voice, and often they don't include any notion of who did the action:

A decision has been made to terminate your employment.

Hey! Who made that decision? You'll never know from the passive-voice statement, because it's written in a style of non-responsibility. Nobody does anything. Things just happen somehow.

People normally use passive voice only about 10 percent of the time; that's a good percentage for your writing, too. Otherwise, you're forcing the reader to decode a sentence structure that's less familiar than the common active-voice structures, and you're possibly writing in a style that evades responsibility. As a result, your proposal is going to seem less convincing, less persuasive, than it would otherwise.

3. *Put the important stuff up front.* One of the most important techniques you can incorporate is what I call "the primacy principle." You might call it "the principle of first impressions," because that's what it boils down to. We tend to take our first experiences as normative. Unconsciously we assume that the things that happen first are the most important. A few years ago, a book for sales professionals stressed the importance of the first five minutes of contact with a client, demonstrating how vital those initial moments are to the future relationship. You probably recognize the truth of this observation intuitively or from your own experience: If you walk into a store and receive rude treatment from a clerk, your opinion of both the store and the clerk will be negative. And it'll probably take a lot of good experiences to change your attitudes.

The same basic principle applies in writing proposals. It's a good idea to try to put the most important facts, information, opinions, or observations up front. This applies to the document as a whole, to sections of a document, to paragraphs, even to sentences.

*Proposals* are easier to use if they're designed from the top down. Start with the most general and most important information, and then narrow the focus to less important material, ending with the least important. Make sure, though, that you're prioritizing the order of information from the reader's point of view, not yours. What matters to your reader may be far different from what matters to you. After all, your orientation may be toward the features or technology of your product or service; the decisionmaker may be more interested in responsiveness to perceived needs, payback periods, delivery schedules, or past experience.

Lengthy documents are always easier to use if they begin with an overview. The overview should provide the reader with a clear statement of the document's purpose, its key content points, and perhaps even the specific action steps being requested. In your proposal, use the cover letter and executive summary to provide this overview.

*Sections of proposals* are easier to read if they begin with summaries of the key points or content. One useful technique is to put a strong selling statement at the outset of each section of a proposal, setting it off by boxing it or by using a distinctive typeface. For example, a section of a proposal that discusses logistics might start with a statement like this:

> The proposed system will be installed and maintained without disrupting current operations and without the use of additional equipment.

The rest of the section would then present the evidence to substantiate that claim. By making the statement first, though, you've told the decisionmaker what you want her or him to think.

*Paragraphs* are easier to understand when they start with a clear topic sentence. This is pretty basic stuff. Most of you were introduced to the concept of topic sentences way back when, probably in the seventh or eighth grade. But since you may have been noticing the opposite sex for the first time about then, it's possible you missed it.

*Sentences* also benefit from an application of the primacy principle, although it's a little more subtle. For example, consider this one:

> Since the sales program cost us nearly $30,000, we obviously were anxious to have everything go well.

This is a crummy sentence, but fairly typical of the kind we see all the time in business writing. It has lots of problems: a weak verb ("were"), vague language ("go well"), ambiguous tone (is the writer pleased or dissatisfied?), vague and pointless modifiers ("nearly," "obviously"). But it also violates the primacy principle.

The reader will perceive whatever comes first in the sentence to be most important. In this instance, the price tag appears up front and may serve to distract the reader from the key point, which is whether our expectations for the program were met. In addition, sentences that begin with a dependent clause are harder to decode because the reader has to hold the dependent clause in limbo until he or she has read the main clause, then go back and see how the two fit together. It's not a big problem, but it does interfere a little with readability.

If the same sentence were rewritten in accord with the primacy principle (and if you were to use a strong verb in the main clause), it would read like this:

> We expected the sales program to be handled in a professional manner, particularly since you charged us $30,000 for it.

In other words, you'd have a sentence that's clearer, more direct, more to the point—a sentence that belongs on the positive side of the ledger.

4. *Apply Sant's Law to every sentence.* What is Sant's Law? Well, in all modesty, it's the most important breakthrough in writing a clear, direct style since the invention of the simple sentence. Okay, maybe I'm not being all that modest, or all that honest, either. But it's a technique that really can help. And it's pretty easy to use.

Here it is in a nutshell: *To write a clear, direct sentence, make sure that your key idea is embedded in the heart of the sentence.*

What's the heart of the sentence? How can you determine whether your key idea is embedded there? If you think back to English class in about the eighth grade, you may have vague memories of being called to the chalkboard to diagram sentences. At the time, you probably thought it was a stupid way to ruin a perfectly good afternoon. I know I did. But it turns out that it can be kind of useful.

Remember the first step in diagramming a sentence? You had to draw a straight, horizontal line. And what went on that line? The subject of the sentence, the verb, and the complement—usually the direct object or indirect object. So suppose you were asked to diagram this sentence:

> The bright red car hit my mother's new pickup truck broadside.

The first thing you would do is draw that line and write down the subject, verb, and complement:

|          car          |        hit        /        truck          |
|-----------------------|-------------------------------------------|

That's the first step and, to apply Sant's Law, the only step you have to take. You probably remember that the rest of the words in that sentence would dangle down below the horizontal line, depending on which part of the sentence they modify. Who cares? All that matters is this: Does the subject/verb/complement communicate the key idea? In this case, yes. A car hit a truck. That's the main point, isn't it?

Perhaps you'll run across a sentence like this in one of your proposals:

> It would appear that enhanced access to the data base on the part of key executives is desirable.

Can you even find the subject and verb in that thing? Well, the subject is "It" and the verb is the ever popular "would appear." Not too exciting, is it?

Try to rewrite the sentence so that the key elements are in the key grammatical slots. Something like this would work:

> Our key executives need better access to the data base.

If you apply Sant's Law, what do you get? The subject is "executives," the verb is "need," and the complement is "access."

> Executives need access . . .

Is that the key idea? I think so.

# *19*

# Editing Your Proposal

So you want to be a good writer? Then force yourself to be a rewriter. That's where good writing happens.

A lot of people apparently believe that good writers don't need to revise, that proposals simply pour out of them in their complete and final forms. Trust me—that's a delusion. And if you currently cling to it, you'll have to give it up. Otherwise, you'll have little chance of improving your work.

How much editing should you do? The correct answer is, as much as you can. But that's no answer at all, because it's so vague.

A related question you might be asking is, how do I edit something I wrote? After all, if I could have done any better, I would have. I've already checked it for misspellings and typos. What's left?

That's a misconception, of course. Checking for misspelling, typos, grammar errors, misplaced punctuation, and so forth is part of editing, but it's not editing. In fact, it's the very last part of editing. Unfortunately, almost nobody learns how to edit in school. Instead, students are threatened with F's if their papers contain more than three misspelled words, so they learn to proofread for spelling mistakes.

## How to Edit

To edit effectively, you must plan the editing process into your management of the overall proposal project. Allow time for it. If possible, divide your time evenly between writing and editing. If you need six hours to write the proposal, allow six hours to edit it, too. Then, build in as much of a buffer as you can between the writing and the editing. In other words, let your writing "cool" before you edit it. You probably already know how difficult it is to edit effectively immediately after you finish writing. Mistakes that you should have noticed just seem to be invisible. Usually, if you look at your proposal right after finishing that first draft, you'll know so clearly what you *meant* to say that you'll be unable to see what you actually *did* say.

Try this: Take your first draft, make a photocopy of it that you can stick in a file, then put the original in an envelope and mail it to yourself. By the time it arrives, you'll have acquired enough detachment from the work to edit it objectively.

Of course, if you don't have a lot of faith in the U.S. mail system, you might just try doing the draft, then spending time on something else. After a couple of days, go back to your draft. Once you've acquired enough detachment to edit effectively, approach the task in four steps.

*Step 1.* Read through the draft quickly and out loud. Listen for rough spots, but don't stop to fix them now. Just put a mark in the margin where things don't sound quite right. As you're reading, ask yourself three questions:

1. Have I written anything obviously dumb? Misplaced modifiers, incomplete thoughts, errors in logic, using the wrong name for the client—all of these qualify as dumb.
2. Have I written with a consistently client-centered focus? Challenge yourself: Is this information necessary? Does it address the client's needs, problems, interests, values?
3. Can I cut material without interfering with the reader's understanding or my own purposes of persuasion? Be ruthless: If it's not contributing to one of the four essentials of a persuasive proposal—evidence you understand the client's problem, a powerfully presented recommendation, evidence of competence to deliver the solution and of your competence to manage the project, and a convincing reason to choose your recommendation over any other—cut it!

*Step* 2. Go back through the proposal more slowly now, and focus on the essential elements:

1. *Audience:* Have I slanted the material toward the audience's
   —Level of expertise?
   —Personality type?
   —Role in the decision-making process?
2. *Purpose*
   —Have I used the persuasive paradigm to structure the proposal as a whole?
   —Have I used it to structure the various sections?
3. *Is the information easy to find?*
   —Did I use logically sequenced sentences, paragraphs, and sections?
   —Are the key ideas up front whenever possible?
   —Are there plenty of highlighting and informative "signposts"?
4. *Is the information easy to understand?*
   —Did I strive for simplicity: in vocabulary, sentence structure, organization?
   —Did I keep the proposal as concise and brief as possible?
   —Was I specific; did I use graphics, and did I provide concrete details and examples (without jeopardizing proprietary information, of course)?
   —Did I check the mechanics: grammar, spelling, punctuation, legibility?
   —Did I keep it interesting and clearly relevant to the reader; is it presented with flair?
5. *Does the total package do the job it's meant to do?*
   —Is the proposal complete and thorough?
   —At the same time, is it focused?
   —Are the contents accurate?
   —Will it arrive on time?

*Step* 3. During the third revision, work on clarity, conciseness, precision, directness, and emphasis. In particular, take a close look at:

1. Word choice
2. Sentence lengths and patterns
3. Readability

If there were spots you marked during your initial reading of the proposal, work on them now. Try rewording them so that they read easier. Take a look at the tips discussed throughout this book. Once you're satisfied with your draft, send it off to be retyped or make the corrections yourself. Get a clean copy and let it sit overnight.

*Step 4.* Now you proofread. Inspect the final copy for mechanical or typographical errors, any of the mistakes of carelessness or neglect. Errors in spelling, punctuation, and grammar and other small mistakes can communicate to a reader that you are careless, hasty, ignorant, or disrespectful. Besides, such mistakes are nothing but background noise that can interfere with your message.

## How Good Is Good Enough?

How much editing should you do? This isn't always an easy question to answer, since you will almost always be limited by the constraints of time or experience in your role as editor. However, if you think about it, what this question is really asking is: "How good is good enough?" When is your proposal good enough to be sent to your audience?

We can define six possible levels of "communication correctness," listing them in order of increasing difficulty of achievement:

1. There are no mechanical, spelling, or punctuation errors and no typos.
2. There are no obvious errors of logic or content that a reader would notice immediately.
3. There are adequate divisions of the material into functional units so that a reader can use the proposal.
4. The presentation is clear and concise, written in a style free of needless jargon, ambiguities, or possible misinterpretations.

5. The presentation is slanted correctly at the primary audience and meets that audience's needs readily.
6. The presentation is thorough, informed, and intelligent, written in a crisp and interesting style, and presented in a format that is easy to use for any possible readers.

So—how good *is* good enough? Most technical or business professionals are satisfied with level 2. If it gets by on the first reading, it's good enough for them.

From the reader's point of view, though, nothing less than level 4 will do. And for a proposal, when the reader is a client or a potential client, you shouldn't tolerate anything less than level 5.

## Measuring Readability

There are several different formulas around that enable you to measure how "readable" your writing is. In fact, some word processors have these formulas built into them, and there are independent software programs available that will check your spelling, grammar, and readability index. But you don't need to invest in any of that, since you can usually do the calculations in your head.

One of the easiest to use is Robert Gunning's Fog Index, which enables you to measure how "foggy"—in other words, how unreadable—a given piece of writing is. The answer you get by using the formula is the school-grade level at which the piece can be read comfortably.

To use the formula, follow these three steps:

1. Count off in the writing sample a passage of about one hundred words, stopping at the period closest to one hundred. Then count the number of sentences in the passage. Divide the total number of words in the passage by the number of sentences. This gives you the average sentence length.

For example: $\dfrac{99 \text{ words}}{3 \text{ sentences}} = 33$ word Average Sentence Length

2. Going back over the same passage, count the number of words having three syllables or more. Do not include:

- Words that are capitalized (proper nouns like *Cincinnati*)
- Words that are combinations of short, easy words (compound words like *bookkeeper* and *understand*)
- Verb forms that are made three syllables by the addition of -*ed* or -*es* or -*ing* (like *created, trespasses, traveling*)

3. Add the numbers representing the average sentence length and the number of words having three syllables or more. Then, to determine the grade scale value of the Fog Index, multiply this sum by .4.

If you're mathematically inclined, you can see that this formula can be written as:

$$.4(ASL + W_{poly}) = \text{Fog Index}$$

where

ASL is the Average Sentence Length

$W_{poly}$ is the number of words with three or more syllables

Readability—whatever else it may be—is a fairly complex phenomenon. Gunning's formula and others can give you a rough numerical value that may or may not be an accurate indicator for a passage's real level of readability. It's possible for a passage to be full of noun clusters, faulty parallel structure, dangling modifiers, vague words, and so on, yet get a good readability score.

However, as a rough guideline, the formulas can be very useful, since they measure the two fundamental components of the reading process: the length of your sentences and the number of big words you're using.

The chart below shows the grade-level correlates for Gunning's Fog Index. Note that grade-level 12 is the danger line. Above that line, reading becomes uncomfortable for the majority of readers. Above level 15, almost nobody is comfortable reading. Remember that this isn't an IQ test. Just because your reader has a Ph.D. doesn't mean you should write at a Fog Index of 20. In fact, almost nobody enjoys reading for extended periods above an index of 10.

| Index | Reading level by grade | Reading level by magazine |
|---|---|---|
| 17 | College postgrad | |
| 16 | College senior | |
| 15 | College junior | (No popular magazine is this difficult) |
| 14 | College sophomore | |
| 13 | College freshman | |
| 12 | High school senior | *Scientific American* |
| 11 | High school junior | *Atlantic Monthly* |
| 10 | High school sophomore | *Time, Newsweek* |
| 9 | High school freshman | *Redbook* |
| 8 | Eighth grade | *Reader's Digest* |
| 7 | Seventh grade | *People* |

# Appendix
# A Proposal Writer's Checklist

I.  The Development Phase

A. Have I analyzed the client's needs thoroughly and creatively?
B. Have I turned the statement of need into an overall strategy?
C. Have I assembled all the necessary information?
D. Have I accurately identified my audience?
   1. Personality style
   2. Level of expertise and familiarity
   3. Role in the decision process
E. Have I storyboarded the overall proposal for continuity and consistency?

II. Style

A. Have I used a natural, friendly tone?
   1. Have I avoided cliches and jargon?
   2. Have I been courteous and tactful?
B. Have I expressed myself clearly?
   1. Do I understand my subject thoroughly?
   2. Are my sentences reasonably short and simple?
   3. Have I used specific words?
   4. Have I adapted my vocabulary to suit the reader?
C. Have I written concisely?
   1. Have I eliminated unnecessary detail?
   2. Have I cut redundancies and solecisms?
D. Have I expressed myself with precision?
   1. Are my ideas in logical and effective order?

    2. Have I analyzed my material and divided it logically into parts?

    3. Have I provided the necessary definitions, details, and examples?

  E. Have I written with proper emphasis?

    1. Did I stick to the main idea?

    2. Does my opening attract interest and attention?

  F. Have I written readable sentences?

III. Structure

  A. Have I chosen an appropriate format for this communication?

  B. Have I structured the communication from the reader's point of view?

  C. Do the discussion sections present the substance of my work clearly?

  D. Have I used a single sentence for each key point and made it stand out to the reader?

IV. Mechanics

  A. Have I included all the necessary mechanical and prose elements needed?

  B. Are my headings and titles clear, properly worded, and parallel?

  C. Have I keyed any tables or figures into the text and discussed them adequately?

  D. Have I proofread the manuscript completely?

# PROPOSAL PLANNING WORKSHEET

Account Executive: _____

Writer(s): _____

_____

Strategy: _____

_____

Format: _____

_____

Completion date: _____

### Audience analysis

1. Who will make the decision on this proposal?
   a. Name(s): _____

   _____

   b. Job title/chief responsibility: _____

   _____

   c. Relationship/attitude toward us: _____

   _____

   d. Background:
      (1) Technical level: _____
      (2) Area of specialization: _____
      (3) Depth of experience: _____
      (4) Personality type: _____
      (5) Role in the decision process _____
2. Are there any secondary audiences? _____

   _____

   _____

# Index

*[Italicized numbers indicate figures.]*